TAPAS

TAPAS

Sensational Small Plates from Spain

···································

BY **JOYCE GOLDSTEIN**

PHOTOGRAPHS BY LEIGH BEISCH

CHRONICLE BOOKS
SAN FRANCISCO

Library of Congress Cataloging-in-Publication Data available.

ISBN 978-0-8118-6298-1

Manufactured in China.

Designed by **ALICE CHAU**.

Prop styling by **SARA SLAVIN**.
Food styling by **SANDRA COOK**.

The photographer wishes to thank her exceptional photo team. Thanks go to Sara Slavin for her incredible props and Sandra Cook for her inspired food and styling. Thank you to Penny Flood, Kate Robinson, and Jeff McLain for their support. Also, special thanks go to Joyce Goldstein and Sara Schneider for allowing me to be a part of another unbelievably wonderful project.

10 9 8 7 6 5 4 3 2 1

Chronicle Books LLC
680 Second Street
San Francisco, California 94107

www.chroniclebooks.com

For Adam and Elena, the Tapas kids.

Muchas Gracias to:

BILL LEBLOND, longtime editor and dear friend
AMY TREADWELL for her eagle eye and organization skills
SHARON SILVA, the goddess of copyediting, at the top of her game, as usual

My son **EVAN** for his excellent wine notes and love of Spanish wine and food, and for encouraging Adam and Elena to taste endless tapas in Spain and at home

Photographer **LEIGH BEISCH** for yet another fabulous set of photos to make you hungry
Food stylist **SARA SLAVIN** for her impeccable eye and taste in props
SANDRA COOK for cooking the food so it looks yummy, and enjoying tasting the results
Designer **ALICE CHAU** for her very clear and elegant design and graphics

LARS KRONMARK for his passion for tapas and our long conversations about Spanish food plus time spent in the kitchen
GREG DRESCHER for inviting me to participate in the extraordinary CIA Worlds of Flavors conferences
JIM PORIS of Food Arts for assigning me the European Pepper powder piece
FOODS OF SPAIN for sending me to Madrid (Jeffrey Shaw, Mercedes Lamamie, Paz Tintore) and for enthusiastic support
KATRIN NAELAPAA of Wines of Spain for all those wonderful tastings
CLARA MARIA DE AMEZUA for her gracious hospitality
CHRIS TRACY of Calphalon for those perfect tapas pans

INTRODUCTION

Ever since my first visit to Spain in 1960, I have been captivated by its cuisine. At the time, the United States had few authentic Spanish restaurants and American cooks had limited access to authentic Spanish food products. I was a lonely culinary cheerleader for the Spanish table, and I struggled to cook its recipes with a combination of traditional and improvised ingredients. In 1984, I opened Square One, a San Francisco restaurant that focused on the foods of the Mediterranean, and I included many Spanish dishes on the menu. Within a year, I was offering a tapas assortment on alternating weekends. These small bites proved a seductive and successful way to introduce new dishes to diners. In my many years as a chef and cooking teacher, I have learned that some cuisines take time to capture the public's imagination—that patience and persistence are required. Slowly but surely, Spain has simmered its way into our culinary consciousness. Nowadays, it is piping hot.

There are many reasons for this heightened awareness: the growth of culinary and cultural tourism, the greater availability of Spanish food products and wines, the press coverage of Spain's avant-garde celebrity chefs, and the growing popularity of tapas. In fact, Spain is now aggressively marketing its products in the United States, and store shelves and Web sites display everything from Spanish olives, olive oil, rice, tuna, and cheeses to chorizo, *serrano* ham, *boquerones*, *membrillo*, Marcona almonds, and wines. In other words, contemporary American cooks can easily find whatever they need to put together a Spanish meal.

Of course, Spanish food has changed over the years, too. Following the decades-long Franco dictatorship, and the consequent stasis in the Spanish kitchen, a quiet culinary revolution took place. It was as if someone had opened the dark, heavy drapes in a living room to let in the sunlight. In the 1970s, a group of chefs in the Basque city of San Sebastián, led by Juan Mari Arzak and inspired by French nouvelle cuisine, created a new and exciting Basque cuisine that stressed lighter dishes, yet did not discard tradition. Their innovation provided the impetus for other Spanish chefs to experiment, and soon chefs around the country were exploring new ways to present their national cuisine. But news of a growing inventiveness in the Spanish kitchen did not reach far beyond the country's borders.

That obscurity changed with the rise of Ferran Adrià in the mid-1980s. This brilliant Spanish chef, with his foams, *gelées*, and liquid nitrogen; his experimental laboratory in Barcelona; and his deconstruction of recipes into components with unexpected textures and temperatures, captured the imagination of the press, the professional culinary establishment, and the dining public. His El Bulli restaurant in Rosas, open only six months each year and famous for its elaborate multicourse menus, is always fully booked, with a long waiting list. Adrià is most often linked to so-called molecular cuisine, a largely chef-centric movement that is impractical for home cooks, and he has inspired many young chefs around the world. Even more important, he has provided Spanish chefs with renewed inspiration to catapult traditional Spanish cooking into the present, with vibrant presentations and fuller, more charismatic flavors.

But after years of waiting in the wings, what finally pushed the Spanish kitchen into the America's culinary spotlight was one of its traditions: tapas. The recent growth of American wine bars and restaurants offering a small-plate menu owes a big debt to Spanish tapas. It is not that Spain invented informal small-plate dining. Indeed, countries all around the Mediterranean are known for their rich assortments of small plates, from Italian antipasti and French hors d'oeuvres to Greek and North African mezes. These new American small-plate restaurants typically reflect that diversity, putting dishes from all of those traditions—and more—on the same menu. But they invariably call their offerings tapas. Even when the menu promises Spanish tapas, the plates often fuse recipes from the Iberian kitchen with those of Latin America.

In these pages, you will find only the tapas of Spain, which are abundant, varied, and delightful, with a focus on traditional plates with deep regional roots. But I have also explored how these time-honored dishes have evolved to yield interesting modern interpretations that continue to respect the past.

A National Institution

Most food scholars agree that the tapas tradition originated in the wine-growing regions of Andalusia, eventually spreading throughout the country. The Moors (Muslim Arabs), who dominated Spain from the beginning of the eighth century until the end of the fifteenth century, settled in the same area, and their meze tradition undoubtedly had an influence on the rise of the tapa.

The word itself comes from *tapar*, "to cover," and Spanish folklore offers its own stories of origin. Among the most popular is that a slice of bread was traditionally set atop a glass of sherry or other wine to prevent any dirt—or some say flies—from tainting the drink. Soon a slice of ham or cheese was added to the bread and the tapa was born. Another tale attributes the birth to a decree by Alfonso X instructing all inns to serve tidbits of food with the wine they poured to ensure against public drunkenness. Regardless of the true origin, the drink accompanied by the snack quickly led to *el tapeo*, essentially the Spanish version of the English pub crawl.

A look at the Spanish dining timetable will help you to understand how tapas dining has evolved into a national institution. Spaniards eat a series of small meals throughout the day and evening. *El desayuno*, or breakfast, is just coffee and a roll, quite early; and then a snack at about 11:00; *la comida*, or the main meal of the day, at 1:30 or 2:00, followed by a siesta; another snack, *la merenda*, at about 5:00, tapas at around 8:00, and a light dinner, *la cena*, at 10:00 or 11:00 or later. With such a schedule, you may wonder when Spaniards find time for work or sleep, and why they are not fat. The Mediterranean diet is undoubtedly what keeps them both energetic and trim.

Between 8 and 10 P.M. in Madrid, Seville, San Sebastián, Barcelona, and other Spanish cities and towns, the tapas crowd hits the streets, where they choose from a variety of different types of establishments. The *bodegón* concentrates mainly on drinks, with a minimum of small plates. The *tasca* is the most popular tapas stop, offering food and drink with equal attention. The *méson* has a tapas bar connected to a restaurant, and the *cervecería* specializes in beer and the foods that pair well with it. In Barcelona, center of *cava* production, there are also *xampanyeries*, Champagne bars that offer small dishes that complement their sparkling wines. House specialties at any of these establishments can number as many as two dozen or more. Some people wander from bar to bar, filling up on delightful and varied small plates, and never sit down to a formal dinner. Even though countless young Spanish chefs are following Ferran Adrià's experimental ways, traditional tapas bars are flourishing because Spaniards don't want to give up their favorite way to eat. They love the informality and the conviviality that comes from sharing. Chefs love tapas, too, because they are an outlet for their creativity.

Tapa Categories

Tapas fall into three major categories: *cosas de picar*, "things to nibble on," or finger food; *pinchos*, food on top of bread held by toothpicks, or food on skewers, served uncooked, grilled, or fried; and *cazuelas* or *cazuelitas*, which require forks and usually have a sauce. A small portion is called a tapa or *media-ración*, and a larger portion is a *ración*.

COSAS DE PICAR represent the broadest category. They include the simplest bowl of marinated olives or fried almonds and pieces of cheese or slices of ham or sausage. Deviled eggs and *tortilla* (omelet) slices are also *cosas de picar*, as are *escabeche* (marinated fish) and *boquerones* (anchovies) cured in olive oil and vinegar. Fried foods, such as *buñuelos* (fritters) and *croquetas* (croquettes), often dipped in *alioli*, and *montaditos* or *tostas* (foods spread on bread [see Shop-and-Serve Tapas, page 37]), fit here as well, along with such classic finger foods as *empanadillas* (bite-sized savory turnovers), *tartaletas* (savory tartlets), and *bocadillos* (small sandwiches).

PINCHOS are foods cooked on skewers or served on toothpicks, and they result in all manner of creative combinations. *Bandarillas* and *palitos*, terms used specifically for foods speared on toothpicks, are typically *pinchos* that are quick and easy to assemble (see Shop-and-Serve Tapas, page 37). (Don't be confused by the term *pintxos*, which is used in the Basque region for all tapas, skewered or not.)

CAZUELAS or **CAZUELITAS** are small-plate versions of larger main dishes, such as *arroz negro* (black rice), *fideuà* (short, fine noodles with seafood), *fabada asturiana* (bean and meat stew), and *piquillos rellenos* (stuffed peppers), and utensils are needed to eat them. Both the vessel and what is cooked and served in it go by the same name.

CAZUELA

The term *cazuela* (or *cassola* in Catalan) comes from the Arabic *qas'ah*, or "bowl." *Cazuelas* are earthenware cooking vessels that come in a variety of shapes and sizes. They retain heat well and can be used in the oven and, with care, on the stove top. They must be seasoned before they are used over direct heat the first time: Soak the *cazuela* in water to cover for 12 hours, and then drain. Next, rub the unglazed base of the interior with 3 garlic cloves, and when the garlic juices have been absorbed, pour in hot water to ½ inch below the rim. Some Spanish cooks also add ½ cup vinegar at this point. Place on a heat diffuser over very low heat and bring slowly to a boil. Simmer until the water is reduced to a scant ½ cup. Discard the water, let the *cazuela* cool slowly, and then wash it if you used vinegar. Dry the *cazuela* well. It is now ready for cooking. (I don't know if the garlic rub is only folklore, but I never ignore such arcane advice, especially when it includes the magic number 3.) For added insurance, you can rub the *cazuela* with olive oil and place in a 300°F oven for about 1½ hours.

Never put boiling liquid into a cold *cazuela*, and never put a hot *cazuela* on a cold surface. Such sudden changes in temperature can cause cracking. *Cazuelas*, which are inexpensive, are sold in many stores specializing in cookware and are available online from such sources as *www.spanishtable.com* and *www.tienda.com*.

How to Recognize a Modern Tapa

In recent years, traditional tapas have had to make room for their modern cousins. Most of these new-comers are easily picked out of a lineup, with presentation the most typical clue. Modern tapas are decoratively arranged on a plate, rather than piled on platters or served in *cazuelas* like their estab-lished counterparts. They also favor precise cutting, with *mirepoix* (¼-inch dice), *brunoise* (⅛-inch dice), and perfect little rounds carved with melon scoops in graduated sizes replacing torn strips or random chunks. A modern ESCALIVADA (page 80), with the egg-plants, peppers, and onions cut into uniform pieces, is a good example. Even chorizo may not be in easily recognizable rounds, but instead in precise squares or rectangles, and seafood such as mussels, clams, and lobsters will be out of their shells, making them less messy to eat.

The deconstruction of ingredients is another clue. The elements of a traditional dish are taken out of the mix and presented separately, offered in dif-ferent combinations, or served at different tempera-tures. Sometimes dishes traditionally served cold are served hot, or dishes have hot and cold elements on the same plate.

A dichotomy is at work here as well: regionalism mixed with an embrace of traditions from elsewhere in the world. Spaniards take great pride in their local products, especially those with denomination of ori-gin (DO) labeling, and in their national dishes rooted in the kitchens of the Moors, ancient Romans, and others. But they are also open to incorporating ideas from beyond their borders, from the ginger and soy of Asia to the ceviches of Latin America to the cheeses of France. For example, in the Basque region, the influence of French cuisine is particularly strong, with foie gras, caviar, smoked salmon, and fish tartare regularly turning up in an assortment of tapas. This mix is not surprising, however. Spain boasted one of the first fusion cuisines, assimilating ideas and products initially from the Romans, Moors, Jews, Phoenicians, Celts, and the New World and later from the Middle East and Far East.

Serving Tapas

In Spain, as elsewhere in the Mediterranean, food always accompanies a beverage. In the case of tapas, sherry or another wine is the most common accompaniment, with beer or hard cider also popular. A glass of wine to a plate of food is considered the proper ratio.

I have included information on pairing wines with tapas (see page 18) and specific recommendations for each recipe, both contributed by my son, Evan Goldstein, a master sommelier since the ripe young age of twenty-six and a man who definitely knows his wine.

Each recipe includes a yield, but the number of servings will primarily depend on how many other tapas you are serving at the same time. The amounts given reflect a meal composed of three or four offerings and serving four to six. Some recipes, such as the CROQUETAS (pages 55 and 58), EMPANADA GALLEGA (page 65), and COCAS (page 69), have larger yields but provide you with great leftovers.

A LITTLE HISTORY

To understand the cuisine of Spain, you need to know a little of its history. From its earliest days, the Iberian Peninsula experienced waves of invaders. Around 1100 BC, the Phoenicians carried their Semitic language and culture to Spain, founding the trading colony of Gadir, now modern Cádiz. In 650 BC, the Celts began streaming across the Pyrenees from the north. Between 500 and 400 BC, the Greeks established colonies on the coast. The Carthaginians started arriving in the sixth century BC and by the middle of the third century BC had conquered much of what is now Spain from North Africa. About 200 BC, the Romans began their conquests in Spain, and after years of fighting the Carthaginians, Greeks, Celts, and Iberian tribes for control, they added the Iberian Peninsula to their growing empire, introducing Christianity to the region in AD 100. Although the Romans established stability in the area, they could not hold on to the territory. In about AD 400, the first pagan Germanic tribes invaded, followed by the total Visigoth conquest around AD 500. Under King Reccared, the entire Iberian Peninsula converted to Christianity, only to fall to the followers of Islam in AD 711.

Within three years, the Moors, Muslims of Arab or Berber descent from North Africa, had extended the boundaries of Islam deep into Spain, Portugal, and across the Pyrenees into France. Their powerful seven-hundred-year presence can be seen architecturally in the mosque of Córdoba, the Alhambra of Granada, and the Alcazar of Seville. In cuisine, their influence is even more all encompassing. During the Dark Ages, when most of Europe struggled to keep civilization alive, philosophy, horticulture, architecture, mathematics, and the culinary arts flourished in Spain and Portugal.

Rebellion against the Muslim rulers was constant, with recurring battles to reclaim the territory from the Moors. In 720, the Christian Visigoths reconquered the Kingdom of Asturias. Sancho III, also known as Sancho the Great of Navarre, set up the Kingdoms of Aragon and Castile, and over the course of successive battles between 1015 and 1028 reduced the great Muslim empire to a series of small provinces.

In 1085, Alfonso VI of Castile, with the help of the Christian Crusaders, recaptured Toledo, and in 1094, Valencia was recaptured from the Moors by El Cid. By 1252, under Ferdinand III, the reconquest of Spain was complete, except for the province of Granada, which eventually fell to Catholic rulers Ferdinand and Isabella in 1492. This significant year, while a triumph for the Catholic monarchs with Columbus's discovery of the New World, also marked the beginning of the expulsion of the country's Jews under the rules of the Inquisition.

All of these various invaders left their cultural and culinary marks on the Iberian Peninsula. The Phoenicians, from their homelands of Lebanon and Syria, brought saffron and planted vineyards. The Romans planted more vineyards, olive trees, and wheat. The Moors initiated the cultivation of rice in Valencia, and planted sugarcane along the eastern Mediterranean coast, while in Andalusia they grew almonds, oranges and lemons (from China), eggplants, spinach, artichokes, and honeydew melons (from Egypt). Quince may have come with the Romans or the Arabs, from its original home in Iran. The Moors also introduced spices such as cumin, coriander, nutmeg, and black pepper into local cooking. The Spanish words for certain foods reflect their Arabic roots: *alcachofa* (artichoke), *almendra* (almond), *azafrán* (saffron), *azúcar* (sugar), *arroz* (rice), *naranja* (orange), *berenjena* (eggplant), and *zanahoria* (carrot). The impact of the Moors on Spanish cuisine remains evident today in such preparations as meat stews with fruit, bread soups, egg-based sweets, and nut-thickened sauces.

While the kitchens of southern Spain were enriched by Moorish customs, northern cooks were influenced by the Celts and Visigoths. Pork, forbidden by Islam, was especially popular, and the Basques, following the lead of the Celts, became important pig farmers, which lead to a tradition of sausage making and the curing of hams.

With the death of King Ferdinand in 1516, the crown passed to Charles V, his grandson. Not long after, an alliance with the powerful house of Hapsburg extended Spanish culinary traditions deep into the heart of Europe. In the sixteenth and seventeenth centuries, Spain ruled both a large part of the Americas and more than half of Europe, and Spanish chefs were eagerly imported by other royal houses. Much of the lofty reputation of Spanish food was built on two factors: the opening of the European spice trade by Spanish and Portuguese sailors and, more important, access to the foods of the New World.

The introduction of New World foods changed forever what Europeans cooked and ate. The conquistadores brought home sweet peppers and chiles, corn, green beans, kidney beans and lima beans, tomatoes, avocados, vanilla, chocolate, papayas, guavas, manioc, pineapples, squashes and pumpkin, pecans, cashews, Brazil nuts, peanuts, potatoes and sweet potatoes, and even turkeys. Not all of these foods were adopted with equal passion, but many of them were, and today Spanish cooks would be lost without their peppers, tomatoes, and eggplants, for example. Spain, in turn, introduced to the New World such now-common foods as sheep, cattle, pigs, goats, chickens, olives, walnuts, wheat, wine, cinnamon, rice, cloves, peaches, apricots, oranges, and coffee.

THE REGIONS OF SPAIN

Spain's varied geography has helped define—and preserve—its rich tradition of regional cuisines. Mountains dominate in the north, open space characterizes the center, and a mix of mountains and valleys, woodlands and shoreline make up the south. The cold waters of the Atlantic rim the north, while the milder Mediterranean laps at the southern and eastern borders.

Regional cooking styles grew out of a time when cooks prepared only what was available nearby, and until the arrival of refrigeration and long-distance transport, food remained intensely local and seasonal. Nowadays, Spanish cooks in every region have access to foodstuffs from around the country and beyond, but regional cuisines, including their typical tapas, have remained distinctive. Because many of the recipes in this book have a strong regional identification, I am including a brief description of the regions of Spain, which I have defined by geography, culture, and history, rather than strict political boundaries, to help you place a tapa in its traditional setting. For information on the wine produced in these regions, see pages 18 to 20.

The North

Cantabria, Asturias, and Galicia, all in the far northwest, reflect strong Celtic influence in their food and culture. Asturias and Cantabria are resplendent with apple orchards, chestnut forests, and lush pastures. Cantabria is known for fine dairy products: butter, cream, yogurt, and soft young cheeses, as well as succulent veal, lamb, and venison. *Boquerones* (anchovies), *angullas* (baby eels), small squid cooked with white beans, and salt cod croquettes are often on the tapas table.

While not known for wine, Asturias is known for its *sidra*, or "cider." Fish cooked with cider as well as chorizo cooked with cider are two signature dishes. Asturias is also home to exceptional white beans, which are popularly combined with both sausages and clams, and to blue-veined cave-aged Cabrales cheese.

Galicia, a mix of hills, mountains, forests, and pasturelands, was once called Cabo Finisterre, or "the end of the earth," because people believed its borders were where the world ended. It is surrounded by the "three seas": the Bay of Biscay to the north, the Atlantic to the west, and the Rias Baixas, a series of river estuaries that indent the southern coastline like the fjords of Norway. Not surprisingly, it is known for its fish—tuna, hake, bream, sea bass, grouper—but it is famous for its shellfish, providing clams, mussels, cockles, crabs, langoustines, and scallops to restaurants all over Spain. Chestnuts, potatoes, peppers, and greens are signature foods, and *empanadas*, big and small, are popular.

The Basque provinces, Spain's easternmost region, boast one of the country's most highly regarded and diverse cuisines. People travel to this prosperous region not only to see the Frank Gehry museum in Bilbao and to enjoy the beaches at San Sebastián, but also to eat. Both cities are home to numerous membership-only gastronomic societies and to many great restaurants, including those of Juan Mari Arzak, Martín Berasategui, and Andoni Luis Adurriz, three international stars. Exceptional dairy products, fine produce, and abundant fish from the Bay of Biscay contribute to a large and interesting repertory of recipes, including a wide variety of tapas, here known as *pintxos*. Basques cooks are known for their *tostas* and *bandarillas*, and annual competitions are held to award prizes for the most interesting tapas.

Aragon, Navarre, and Rioja are neighboring regions that lie close to France. The land falls from the Pyrenees to the calm Ebro River basin farther south, and is planted with wheat, vineyards, fruit orchards, and such vegetables as beans, artichokes, and asparagus. This is the zone of peppers, which are widely used in the dishes of all three regions. The mountainous north produces lamb of exceptional quality; the town of Tudela, in Navarre, is famous for its large asparagus; and the chorizo of Rioja and the air-cured ham of Aragon, both commonly used in tapas, are renowned throughout the country.

The Center

The two Castiles, traditionally known as Old Castile and New Castile, occupy most of Spain's great central plateau. Old Castile (Castile and Léon), which extends from Cantabria in the north to Avila in the south, was first to be recaptured from the Moors in the ninth century, thus its name. Bean and meat *cocidos* (stews) are the mainstay of the cuisine in both its major cities—Salamanca, Valladolid, Segovia, Burgos, León—and in its vast countryside. Old Castile is also dubbed *la zona de los asados*, or "the zone of the roasts," simply cooked suckling lamb, pig, or goat.

New Castile, also known as Castile-La Mancha, embraces the area from Madrid at its northern border to the southern town of Valdapeñas and the Sierra Morena range, which divides it from Andalusia. *La mancha* comes from the Arabic *manhsa*, or "dry land," and today wheat, chickpeas, and lentils are cultivated on the area's vast plains. New Castile is also the center of Spanish saffron cultivation. Lamb, game birds, and trout are menu staples. Madrid is the area's major city, with Toledo, Aranjuez, and Valdepeñas important secondary cities. Old and New Castile have similar cuisines: both are *cocido* territory. You will also find the famed TORTILLA ESPAÑOLA (page 50), *buñuelos de queso*, ENSALADA DE PATATAS (page 78), and ALBÓNDIGAS (page 150) here. And because the region is known for its bread, MONTADITOS (page 44) and bocadillos (sandwiches) are also popular.

Extremadura is on the extreme western edge of Spain, adjacent to the mountainous Portuguese border, with Andalusia to the south and Old and New Castile to the north and east, respectively. Sparsely populated, it is a land of chestnut, oak, and beech forests alternating with upland pastures inhabited by flocks of sheep and herds of cattle and with seemingly endless prairies. Wild asparagus (*trigueros*) and wild mushrooms for cooking *al ajillo* flourish here. But Extremadura is best known for its exceptional air-cured ham and chorizo, the product of pigs that roam the oak forests. Both carry denomination of origin labeling and are prized on the tapas table. It is also the region that produces *pimentón de la Vera*, the smoky paprika that is becoming a pantry staple in many kitchens outside of Spain, and *torta del Casar*, a creamy sheep's milk cheese that can be eaten with a spoon when perfectly ripe. Prosperous Tierra de Barros, a region in southern Extremadura, gets its name from its rich cache of reddish clay (*barro*), which is used in making the *cazuelas* sold throughout the country.

The South

Andalusia—from al-Andalus, its name during the Moorish occupation—is rich in both history and cuisine. In fact, when most people think of Spain, it is an image of Andalusia that comes to mind. Its architecture is striking: whitewashed villages, the Moorish mosque-turned-cathedral in Córdoba, the Alcazar palace and Giralda tower in Seville, and the Alhambra, with its bubbling fountains and sun-dappled Moorish courtyards, in Granada. There are olive, orange, and almond orchards and vineyards devoted to grapes for making the area's famed sherry. Not surprisingly, most Andalusian cuisine shows a strong Moorish influence, with its gazpachos, nut sauces, and sweet desserts. There is also a strong tradition of fried foods, especially around Cádiz, where TORTILLITAS DE CAMARONES (page 62) are popular, and of kebabs, another nod to the Moors.

The Mediterranean Coast

Catalonia has its own language and a distinctive style. It is made up of four provinces, Gerona, Lerida, Tarragona, and Barcelona. Barcelona is its cultural heart, known for its Antonio Gaudí architecture, the famed Ramblas for walking, high-tech housewares shops and high fashion, and the Miró and Picasso museums. The city is also a diner's paradise, with great restaurants found throughout its neighborhoods. Catalan cuisine is a bonanza for cooks and food scholars, with hundreds of classic dishes and countless small regional variations, as well as avant-garde interpretations of the classics. A trio of Catalan sauces, ALIOLI (page 30), SALSA ROMESCO (page 32), and SAMFAINA (page 34), regularly show up at tapas bars, as do ARROZ NEGRO (page 127), ESCALIVADA (page 80), and BERENJENAS RELLENAS A LA CATALANA (page 96).

The Levante, which looks eastward to the Mediterranean, comprises two autonomous communities, Valencia and Murcia. Rice, sugarcane, oranges, lemons, tangerines, peaches, figs, and apricots are cultivated, and large commercial market gardens, called *huertas*, produce a wide variety of vegetables—peas, fava beans, artichokes, green beans, turnips, tomatoes, peppers—year-round. The region, and especially its major city, Valencia, is well known for rice dishes, such as paella and *arroz a la marinera*, and for salt cod served as a spread at tapas bars.

The Islands

The Canary Islands, a group of ten volcanic islands (three uninhabited) just off the coast of North Africa, were taken over by Spain in 1402. Fruits—dates, bananas, oranges, figs, pineapples—thrive in the subtropical climate, and fish dishes, not surprisingly, fill local menus. Island cooks are particularly celebrated for their *mojos*, sauces made in red (paprika) or green (parsley or cilantro) versions and used for accompanying tapas and other dishes.

The Balearics, which include two major islands, Majorca and Minorca, and three smaller ones, Cabrera, Ibiza, and Formentera, lie in the Mediterranean, beyond Valencia. Olives, almonds, and tropical fruits are cultivated, and the local cuisine shows a strong Catalan influence. Like on the Canaries, fish are important menu staples, as are a pair of signature sausages, *sobrasada* and *butifarra*, made from the local *porc negre*, or "black pig." You will find them at tapas bars, along with the islands' famed *cocas*, pizzalike flat breads.

WHAT TO DRINK WITH TAPAS

BY EVAN GOLDSTEIN

The Spanish equivalent of America's hot dogs, beer, and football is tapas, wine, and conversation. It is not that the Spanish aren't passionate about their *futbol* (soccer), it's just that they embrace the *sport* of eating, drinking, and talking even more.

Enjoying tapas with wine is a time-honored tradition in Spain, a national pastime that helps define the character of the country. In other words, stopping at a few tapas bars in the early evening—known as *de tapeo*, or barhopping—is as much about the Spanish lifestyle as it is a source of sustenance.

These small plates are all over the country, but four centers of tapas dining stand out: the Basque Country (specifically San Sebastián), Andalusia (the land of sherry), and the cities of Barcelona and Madrid. Not surprisingly, all of them, with the exception of Madrid, are also significant wine areas. The Spanish dine late, usually sitting down around ten, so the pre-meal inevitably begins around eight or so in a tapas bar, or *taparia*. Nearly every bar turns out variations on classic plates, but each establishment is usually known for a specific dish as well. In my explorations of Spain's tapas bars, locals are always quick to point out that the best way to enjoy the evening is to head out to a small number of bars, in sequence, enjoying the specialty at each bar before moving on to the next stop. However, what you drink at the bars is less specific.

The most important thing to remember when selecting a beverage to accompany tapas is to avoid overthinking your choice. It is *just* tapas and wine, consumed in a tapas bar, with the focus on social interaction. Spaniards are not contemplating if the acidity of a *cava* is high enough to cut through the richness of a *torta*, or if the tannins in a *reserva* from Rioja are appropriate with a *bocadillo de jamón serrano*. That approach defeats the purpose of tapas, which are more about getting together than drinking fine wines. In fact, most Spanish tapas bars offer no more than about a dozen wines, and from what I have seen, their customers are satisfied with that number of choices. Also, folks who eat tapas consume myriad other beverages with them, too, from beer to cider to *orujo* (Spanish grappa) to mineral water to soda. It isn't just about wine.

But while these nonwine choices are prevalent and enjoyed by many, this book celebrates the classic pairing of wine and tapas. That choice has refined my focus to defining which wine styles within the following broad categories work best with tapas.

SPARKLING WINES: Effervescence is not unique to sparkling wine. Many Spanish white wines are fresh and somewhat *pétillant*, and beer and cider are also spritzy. The quality is appreciated in all of these cases because it cleanses the palate and stimulates the appetite, making effervescent beverages a popular choice in *taparias*. Within the category of these *vinos espumosos*, *cava* reigns above all. In fact, one is hard-pressed to find much else. *Cava*, both a wine and the Catalan appellation of the lion's share of the production, is a well-made, delightfully inexpensive, and enjoyable alternative to table wines and goes down easy with a variety of tapas.

WHITE WINES: Perhaps the greatest strides in Spanish winemaking over the past few decades have been made in white wines. Tapas bars invariably feature what is "local" and "fresh." While Andalusia defers to dry sherry (see fortified wines, following), the Basque Country has its beloved Txacolina, central Spain celebrates Rueda (based on the Verdejo grape), and Galicia boasts the wildly popular Albariño or Albariño-based bottlings. Throughout Rioja, a local Viura-based wine is a good match, and tapas eaters in Barcelona look to a refreshing choice from somewhere in surrounding Catalonia. While there is considerable range and diversity in all of these bottles, they share a zesty, vibrant, and almost crunchy acidity that pairs well with tapas.

ROSÉ WINES: Long before the fad of dry rosés became fashionable, the Spanish were guzzling their *rosados* with zeal. Traditionally, Navarre has been the most renowned source of these food-friendly blush wines, which are redolent of red-wine fruit and carry the crisp refreshment of a white wine. Served with a cool snap to bring out their flavor, they are among Spain's most accommodating wine offerings, flexible with fish, meat, cheese, chorizo, and ham. They are most readily found in cities and towns with nearby wine regions that produce them. In addition to Navarre, look to Rioja, La Mancha, and Castile and León.

RED WINES: Generally these wines tend to be *joven*, or unoaked styles that are fruit forward and generous in the mouth, go down easily, and are neither overly tannic nor alcoholic. Those qualities mean you can enjoy them with a wide range of dishes. Whether they are local wines of place (Rioja throughout the eponymous region, Ribera del Duero wines in Castile and León, and so on) or simply delicious table wines coming from the regions of La Mancha, Catalonia, or Valencia, they are great tablemates. Wines that have seen some barrel aging are labeled *crianza* and may well be the premium offering at an *taparia*, though some establishments may also serve *reserva* wines, with additional oak and bottle age.

FORTIFIED WINES: The realization of these wines depends on a method of vinification that includes the light addition of neutral grape distillate as part of its defining style. The most common fortified wine in Spain, sherry is native to the Jerez district of Andalusia, the region that is also typically credited with being the ancestral home of the tapas bar. Consumed chilled and by the bottle, dry sherry—mostly fino and manzanilla—is a wonderful and uniquely Spanish way to enjoy tapas. Contrary to conventional thinking, fino and manzanilla sherries are rarely above 15 to 16 percent alcohol, making them relatively light and food friendly. For richer fare, traditional amontillado sherry is ideal, while dishes with a sweet edge pair nicely with sweeter, denser olorosos. Finally, fortified wines from Montilla-Moriles, which lies inland from Jerez, share a similar style and terminology to sherry. They are more difficult to locate, but if found, they are a tasty alternative. This is also true of Málaga, originating around the city of the same name, but for sweet styles only.

In the recipes that follow, I have provided both Spanish recommendations and non-Spanish alternatives in case the Spanish choice(s) are unavailable or you would prefer to go beyond Spain's borders. The wines, both Spanish and not, are articulated by grape first and denominated region of origin (DO) second. For example, Mencía BIERZO within Spain refers to a red wine made from the Mencía grape in the DO of Bierzo. A Tempranillo from Rioja or Albariño from Galicia follows the same logic. Some wines, like sherry in Andalusia, are the wine and style—manzanilla sherry or fino sherry, for example—in an appellation (Jerez). Others wines may be listed as blends, such as Tempranillo/blend RIBERA DEL DUERO. This refers to a Tempranillo-dominated blended wine (in this case, Cabernet Sauvignon or Merlot might be part of the blend) from Ribera del Duero.

The listing of non-Spanish wines follows a similar logic, which is easy in New World wines, such as Zinfandel from California, but can be a little more confusing in Old World wines outside Spain. For example, a Cabernet Franc from the Loire Valley of France doesn't say Chinon or Borgeuil, though that is what may be meant.

Whichever wine path you choose to travel, Spanish or non-Spanish, your palate will be well rewarded. As Spaniards say, "¡Que aproveche!"

THE SPANISH PANTRY

Because I am a responsible consumer and a careful cook, I want to know where my food comes from and how it is raised. I believe in supporting local farmers and local artisanal food producers. I look for meat and poultry that is free of hormones and antibiotics, and for fish and shellfish caught or raised by eco-friendly means. But when cooking the food of Spain, I also want to enjoy the taste of the *terroir*—the unique geography of flavor that only a Spanish product can deliver. That is why I stock my pantry with selected Spanish ingredients, many of them from artisanal producers and with a *denominacion de origen* (DO) label that guarantees care in production.

Fortunately, many of my local markets carry Spanish olive oil, rice, cheeses, sherry vinegar, Marcona almonds, smoked paprika, and saffron. Some even stock chorizo from Palacios and *serrano* ham from Redondo Iglesias, two excellent producers. For these and other items that you cannot find easily where you live, keep in mind three online sources: *www.tienda.com*, *www.spanishtable.com*, and *www.zingermans.com*. All of them carry many of the following items.

Olive Oil

The Romans introduced the olive tree to the Iberian Peninsula, and today about four thousand square miles of Spain are given over to olive cultivation, with some 92 percent of the crop used for making olive oil. Numerous varieties are used in oil production, with Picual, Hojiblanca, Lechin, and Arbequina among the best known. The Spanish Ministry of Agriculture has demarcated extra virgin oils from several regions: so look for the DO on the label when shopping for oil. The most productive regions are Baena, in the province of Córdoba; Sierra de Segura, in the province of Seville; and Borjas Blancas and Siurana, in Catalonia. Some of the best producers are Nuñez de Prado, Columela, L'Estornell, and Unio.

In general, Catalan oils are made from Arbequinas and are relatively light, with a hint of almond and dried fruit. Andalusian oils are primarily made from Picual and Picudo olives and are more forward and olivey in flavor. Oils from Seville, Málaga, and Córdoba, fashioned mostly from Hojiblanca olives, are almondy and a bit peppery, while oils from Bajo Aragon, Tarragona, and the Balearics, pressed principally from Empeltre olives, are light and mild. Finally, Cornicabra olives are popular in Toledo and Castile-La Mancha, where the oils are commonly smooth, sweetly pungent, and greenish gold.

Olives

Green olives in Spain are typically pickled in a spiced brine, with some pitted and stuffed with pimientos, anchovies, or almonds. Black olives are usually treated to a mixture of olive oil, vinegar, and herbs, with strips of citrus peel sometimes added. New-crop olives appear on the market just before Christmas. Look for the small green Arbequina from Catalonia, the Picual from Andalusia, the small green Manzanilla from Extremadura, the medium-size black Empeltre from Aragon, the Aloreña from Málaga, and the big, greenish brown Obregon from Andalusia.

Sherry Vinegar

Made from Palomino grapes, the best sherry vinegar comes from traditional sherry producers in Jerez de la Frontera, in Andalusia. It undergoes two natural fermentations and is then aged by the traditional *solera* system used in making sherry: vinegars from different vintages are slowly shifted down from the top barrels that hold the newest vinegar into the bottom barrels that hold the oldest. Sherry vinegar is nutty, a bit sweet but not as sweet as balsamic, and smooth, with just a trace of oak. Look for the word *reserva* on the label, which tells you the vinegar is aged. Other Spanish vinegars are made from *cava*, *moscatel*, and red and white wines.

Peppers

Peppers were unknown in Europe until the conquistadores brought them back from South America, and nowadays, because of crossbreeding and selection, many pepper varieties are grown in Spain that are not grown elsewhere. Spanish cooks use bell peppers, but also rely on a number of specialty peppers.

ÑORAS, which are grown in Murcia in southeast Spain, are small, round, sweet brick-red peppers, usually dried and sometimes ground. They are used whole or shredded, typically in stews, and are similar to the three-inch-long smoky-sweet *choriceros*, peppers that vary depending on locale and take their name from their original use as a seasoning for chorizo.

PIMENTÓN, or paprika, is a signature flavor component in Spanish cooking, used to color sausages, stews, and soups. Spanish paprika is similar to Hungarian paprika but is deeper red and less finely ground. *Pimentón de la Vera* is a stone-ground smoked paprika available in three types: *dulce*, or "sweet"; *agridulce* or "bittersweet"; and *picante*, or "hot." It comes from the region of Extremadura and carries DO status. The signature smoky flavor comes from slowly drying the peppers in racks suspended over smoldering oak fires, a process that takes about two weeks. Not all Spanish paprika is smoked, however. In Murcia, dried *ñoras* are ground to yield an unsmoked sweet *pimentón*. La Odalisca, Chiquilin, and El Ruiseñor all produce good-quality unsmoked paprika.

PIQUILLO PEPPERS, grown in Navarre, are deep red and have a bittersweet, not hot, flavor. Their name, which means "little beak," comes from their pointed, triangular profile. Harvested primarily in October and roasted over beech wood, the best peppers are peeled by hand and packed in their own juices in jars or cans. They are ideal for stuffing but are also served drizzled with oil and a little sherry vinegar for an easy tapa (see Shop-and-Serve Tapas for more ideas).

ROMESCO, which is rarely exported, is a small dried pepper used to flavor the classic Catalan nut-thickened sauce of the same name. The ancho chile is a reasonable substitute.

Saffron

A signature spice of Spain, saffron, or *azafrán* in Spanish, takes its name from the Arabic *za'faran* (*zafra* means "yellow"). The world's most expensive spice, it is the dried stigmas of a type of purple crocus, and it takes tens of thousands of plants to yield a pound of saffron threads. Introduced to Spain and Portugal from Asia Minor by the Moors, and planted in Andalusia, Valencia, and southern Castile, saffron should be purchased in threads, or filaments, rather than in powder form.

Most recipes call for steeping saffron threads in boiling or very hot liquid, such as wine, water, or stock, to develop their flavor and color before adding them to a dish. If a recipe does not call for steeping the threads, you can release their flavor by warming them, either in a dry pan over low heat or on a plate in a microwave oven for about 30 seconds, and then crushing them in a mortar with a pestle. Saffron imparts a golden hue to food. Look for Spain's La Mancha brand, which boasts deep red threads.

Rice

The Byzantines reportedly brought rice to Spain, but it was the Arabs who introduced large-scale rice production to the Levante region of Valencia. Cultivation eventually spread to the Ebro River delta, to the marshlands around the Guadalquivir River in the south of Andalusia, and to the Calasparra region near Murcia. Given the Arab preference for sweetness, the earliest written rice recipes show it cooked in milk with sweet spices, with the first savory recipe—rice cooked in meat broth—not appearing in a book until the sixteenth century. By the eighteenth century, rice had become a Spanish pantry staple. Spanish rice is short or medium grain. In Calasparra, which has DO status, both Balilla and Bomba varieties are harvested, with the former in greater production. Bomba is also cultivated in Valencia and the Ebro River delta. Italian Arborio rice can be substituted in a pinch.

Cured Meats

Read the label on Spanish cured meats closely. *Serrano* and *ibérico* chorizos from Spain are available, primarily under the Palacios brand. Most of the other meat products you find in markets or online are produced by Spaniards in this country, many of them by La Española Meats of Los Angeles.

HAM Spain produces superb cured hams. *Jamón serrano* is a cured Spanish ham similar to *prosciutto di Parma*, but a bit more intense and gamy. Redondo Iglesias is a popular brand. Before the outbreak of swine fever and the massive slaughter of domestic animals during the Civil War, all of the *serrano* hams came from the native *ibérico* pig, also known as *pata negra*, which roamed freely, feeding on acorns (*bellotas*) in the oak forests of Andalusia and Extremadura. Today, only 5 percent of all the *serrano* hams come from this prized pig distinguished by its black hooves. The best-known hams with DO status are Jabugo, Cortegana, and Cumbres

Mayores in the Sierra de Aracena in the province of Huelva. Those from Teruel in Aragon and Guijuelo in the province of Salamanca, where the famed Joselito ham is produced, are also well regarded. In early 2008, the long-awaited *jamón ibérico* became available in the United States. Not surprisingly, it is quite expensive.

PORK LOIN In tapas bars, dry-cured pork loin, called *lomo curado* or *lomo embuchado* is served much like *jamón serrano*, thinly sliced. It is typically cured with salt, garlic, and paprika.

Sausages

Do not confuse Mexican chorizo, which is uncooked and seasoned with different spices and vinegar, with cured Spanish chorizo. The latter is usually pork and easily recognized by its red color—from paprika—and its uniquely Spanish mix of spices, herbs, and garlic. There are numerous versions of chorizo, and the style varies from dry (such as *chorizo de Pamplona*) to semicured (such as *chorizo de Bilbao*), from medium grind to coarse grind, from mild to hot, depending on the region. At tapas bars, chorizo is usually served simply sliced or in a small sandwich and occasionally in a stew.

MORCILLA is blood sausage, and like chorizo, it varies depending on the region. Some versions include rice and/or onions, others are flavored with spices or are laced with nuts and raisins, and still others are smoked. At tapas bars, the sausages are usually sliced and fried. They are also popular additions to bean stews. Spanish blood sausages sold in the United States are produced domestically.

SOBRASADA is a specialty of the Balearic Islands, especially Majorca. It is a soft, thick sausage made from minced lean pork and pork belly and is a coral color from the addition of paprika. It makes a tasty tapa spread on bread.

BUTIFARRA comes in two types: white and dark. The delicate white pork sausage is usually scented with cinnamon and cumin, while the dark sausage includes blood. Some of the best examples comes from Vich, a town in the Pyrenees. *Butifarra* is also popular in Majorca.

LONGANIZA is the name given to cured thin sausages made from minced and marinated pork. Those from Navarre and Aragon are usually sliced and eaten with bread or fried. They are also added to *revueltos* (scrambled eggs) and *tortillas*.

Seafood

Spanish cooks use a variety of excellent seafood and seafood products for making tapas. Many of them are imported to the United States, or similar products from elsewhere can be used if a Spanish label cannot be found.

ANCHOVIES Spanish anchovies, known variously as *anchoas* and *boquerones*, are eaten all over Spain, but the finest ones come from the Basque region. They are eaten both fresh—usually fried—and preserved. White fillets preserved in vinegar and olive oil, sold in cans and sometimes plastic tubs at gourmet markets and Spanish and Italian delicatessens, frequently appear on tapas bar menus. Even though they are preserved, they are often simply labeled either *boquerones en vinagre* or white anchovies, so I am calling them *boquerones* in these pages. Anchovies canned in olive oil are also used.

SALT COD Found in pantries all over Spain, salt cod is popularly used in everything from tapas to salads to main courses. Look for uniform white fillets imported from Spain and usually sold in Spanish and Italian delicatessens. The salt cod packed in wooden boxes comes from Canada and is usually not as pale as European salt cod, and some of the pieces can be quite thin and ragged.

All salt cod must be soaked in a few changes of cold water before using. The soaking time will depend on the thickness of the pieces. A piece about 1½ inches thick will take 36 to 48 hours to rehydrate, changing the water three or four times.

SQUID INK Used for making ARROZ NEGRO (page 127) and other dishes, squid ink (*tinta de calamar*) comes in 4-gram packets and can be refrigerated almost indefinitely. If it seems dry when you go to use it, soak the packet in warm water to loosen it up.

TUNA Superb tunas are caught in the cold waters of the Bay of Biscay and packed in olive oil in jars or cans labeled *bonita del norte* or *atún claro*. Look for Ortiz brand, or, if unavailable, seek the Italian Genova brand, the Sicilian Flot brand, or other good-quality olive oil–packed tuna. *Mojama*,

CLEANING SQUID

Squid turns up in countless guises in tapas bars, and Spanish cooks make quick work of cleaning it for cooking. Many fishmongers carry already-cleaned squid, but cleaning it yourself takes relatively little time, saves money, and gives you a better chance to choose the size squid you need.

To clean a squid, pull the head from the body. Cut off the tentacles just above the eyes, and then push out the little round hard piece (the "beak") from the base of the tentacles and discard. Set the tentacles aside. With a flat side of a knife, push down on the body of the squid to push out the innards. Discard them, and then reach into the cavity and pull out the quill-like cartilage and discard. Scrape or pull away the mottled skin covering the body. Rinse the body and tentacles well, pat dry, and leave whole or cut as directed in individual recipes.

salt-dried tuna loin produced mainly around Cádiz, home of Spain's annual tuna catch, is another tuna product that is turned into tapas, often thinly sliced and drizzled with olive oil or paired with onion or *piquillo* peppers. The tuna is filleted in long strips, salted, rinsed, and dried in the sea air for about three weeks. *Huevas de atún*, or salted tuna roe, is similar to the *bottarga* of Italy and is typically shaved or grated atop salads. The salted roe of lingcod and grey mullet are also popular. *Bottarga* can be substituted.

Cheeses

Cheeses are most often a dessert course in Spain, usually paired with fresh fruit, *membrillo* (quince paste), dried figs, dates, or almonds or drizzled with honey. But they are also an important element of the tapas table, served either plain in slices or in simple combinations with other foods. Here is a handful of popular choices when serving tapas.

MANCHEGO is the best-known Spanish cheese. Made from sheep's milk in New Castile, it is rich, complex, and slightly grainy and is aged for a minimum of two months. It is sold in three grades: *fresco*, the youngest, ivory colored and still somewhat elastic; *curado*, aged about thirteen weeks with a firm center and deeper yellow; and *añejo*, matured for seven months to one year, darker, harder, and more sharply flavored. Some may be aged as long as two years. It is produced in large rounds, in the past with a rind imprinted with the esparto-grass baskets in which it was aged. Nowadays, the pattern is the product of a plastic basket.

TETILLA is a creamy, young cone-shaped cheese from Galicia made from pasteurized cow's milk. It has a slightly elastic texture and mildly tangy flavor.

ZAMORANO is a slightly salty sheep's milk cheese from Castile, with a moderately grainy, firm texture and a relatively sharp, yet still buttery flavor. Aged for about six months, it is cylindrical and sports a dark rind—the result of frequent rubbing with olive oil—with a herringbone pattern.

IDIAZÁBAL is a Basque sheep's milk cheese with a big nutty flavor, a smooth texture, and a dark brown rind. Both young and aged and smoked and plain versions are available.

CABRALES is a blue-veined cheese aged in caves in Asturias. Made from cow's milk or from sheep's and goat's milk and with a yellow-brown rind, it is a soft to medium-firm, sharply flavored, slightly acidic, rich cheese reminiscent of Roquefort or Gorgonzola.

MAHÓN is made from cow's milk with 45 percent butterfat. Produced in Menorca, in the Balearics, it is traditionally shaped into a round-cornered square in cheesecloth and aged from about one month up to a year. As it ages, the creamy, white center becomes harder, sharper, and darker.

TORTA DEL CASAR is a soft, ripening sheep's milk cheese from Extremadura with a pungent taste. It is typically eaten by cutting away the top and scooping out the creamy, runny center.

REQUESÓN is a soft, fresh curd cheese similar in texture to ricotta. It is not exported but similar curd cheeses may be found in markets that specialize in Latin American foods, or ricotta may be used in its stead.

Quince Paste

This terra-cotta-colored fruit confection, known as *membrillo* or *dulce de membrillo*, is made by simmering quinces with sugar over low heat until reduced to a thick purée that is then dried. The resulting rich paste, which is solid enough to slice and is sold in bricks or blocks, is a common accompaniment to Manchego cheese in tapas bars.

SPANISH COOKING TERMS

These four culinary terms—two flavor bases and two cooking techniques—are common not only to tapas recipes but also to all Spanish cuisine.

SOFRITO combines chopped onions and minced garlic and cooks them very slowly in olive oil until golden and soft. Chopped tomatoes and sometimes chopped parsley are added as the onion and garlic cook. The mixture eventually cooks down to a rich, thick purée. The quantity for each element varies according to individual recipes.

PICADA is a mixture used to thicken and flavor Spanish sauces, particular in Catalonia. Ingredients vary depending on the recipe, but you might find almonds, hazelnuts, pine nuts, bread, garlic, saffron, cinnamon, bitter chocolate, or parsley in the mix. The elements are traditionally pounded to a smooth paste in a mortar, although today a small food processor is the more likely tool, and then stirred into the sauce toward the end of cooking.

A LA PARILLA, sometimes called *a la bras*, describes cooking meat on a grid over a charcoal fire. The heat is intense and the food is seared quickly on the outside, retaining juices and moisture. Food cooked *a la parilla* should be turned with tongs, rather than pierced with a fork, so as not to release precious juices.

A LA PLANCHA refers to cooking meat or fish over very high heat on a thick metal griddle or hot plate. The sizzling-hot surface is lightly brushed with olive oil to prevent sticking. As with foods cooked *a la parilla*, tongs, not a fork, are used for turning. A cast-iron griddle or skillet can be used for recipes that specify cooking *a la plancha*.

The sauces that follow originated in specific Spanish regions but today are served all over the country, in homes, restaurants, and tapas bars. They are typical accompaniments to many of the dishes in this book.

FIVE BASIC SAUCES

ALIOLI   30
GARLIC MAYONNAISE

SALSA ROMESCO   32
PEPPER AND NUT SAUCE

SAMFAINA   34
MIXED-VEGETABLE SAUCE

MOJO VERDE Y MOJO COLORADO   35
GREEN SAUCE AND RED SAUCE

ALIOLI

GARLIC MAYONNAISE

Alioli, which was introduced to Spain by the Romans, is equally claimed by Levante and Catalonia. It is used for dipping or for spreading with a variety of tapas, including FRITOS (page 46), BUÑUELOS DE BACALAO (page 60), MONTADITOS (page 44), fish and shellfish, rice and noodles, meat, and vegetables. In some parts of Catalonia, it is enhanced by the addition of honey, ground walnuts, or puréed quince, apples, or pears. The fruit versions are served with grilled or roasted meats, chicken, rabbit, and even with CROQUETAS DE JAMÓN Y QUESO (page 55).

Originally, no eggs were used in the sauce. Instead, garlic was crushed to a paste with salt and then mixed with olive oil and thickened with a small amount of bread crumbs. But the emulsion is quite fragile and you need a good deal of elbow grease to produce a successful version that doesn't break. Nowadays, egg yolks are added, which simplifies the preparation and turns the sauce into a garlic mayonnaise. The egg yolk version can be made in a mortar with a pestle, the traditional tools, or more easily in a food processor. In either case, all of the ingredients should be at room temperature. The flavor of most extra virgin olive oil is too strong for an all-purpose sauce, so I advise a milder virgin or pure olive oil, or a mixture of extra virgin olive oil and canola oil. The oil must be added drop by drop (a plastic squeeze bottle works well) while beating—or processing—constantly until an emulsion forms. You can then add the balance of the oil in a thin, steady stream.

MAKES ABOUT

1¾

CUPS

1 tablespoon garlic, finely chopped (about 6 cloves)

Kosher salt

2 large egg yolks

3 to 4 tablespoons fresh lemon juice

About 1½ cups pure olive oil, or ¾ cup each extra virgin olive oil and canola oil

1   Have all of the ingredients at room temperature. If the garlic cloves have a green sprout at their center, cut it away (it imparts a bitter flavor), and then finely chop enough garlic to measure 1 tablespoon. In a mortar, combine the garlic and a big pinch of salt and grind with a pestle to a fine paste.

2   Drop the egg yolks into a blender or food processor. Add 1 to 2 tablespoons lemon juice and process until blended. With the machine running, add the olive oil, a few drops at a time, until the mixture begins to emulsify, and then keep adding the oil until the mixture is the consistency of a thick mayonnaise. Pulse in most of the garlic. Pulse in the remaining lemon juice and more garlic and salt to taste.

3   Transfer to a tightly covered container and refrigerate until needed.

QUINCE VARIATION

Whisk about ½ cup puréed cooked quince or smooth quince jam into the finished *alioli*, and balance the flavor with a little fresh lemon juice. Or, heat *membrillo* (quince paste) with enough water to create a purée, whisk to combine, and then let cool completely before adding to the *alioli*.

APPLE VARIATION

Whisk about ½ cup puréed cooked apple into the finished *alioli*, and balance the flavor with a little fresh lemon juice.

RED PEPPER VARIATION

Seed and purée 1 roasted red bell pepper or 4 *piquillo* peppers and whisk into the finished *alioli*. Balance the flavor with a little fresh lemon juice, and add sweet paprika to taste, if desired. If you want a bit of heat add some hot paprika as well. And if you want a smoky undertone, use sweet *pimentón de la Vera*.

SAFFRON VARIATION

Steep about 30 saffron threads in 1 tablespoon boiling or very hot water until cool, about 15 minutes. Whisk the saffron and its steeping liquid into the finished *alioli*.

SALSA ROMESCO

PEPPER AND NUT SAUCE

Romesco is the name for a pepper, a seafood dish, and this rich and flavorful nut-thickened sauce, a specialty of the Catalan city of Tarragona. Traditionally, the sauce is served as a condiment for cooked shellfish and grilled wild green onions. I call it "Catalan ketchup" because it seems to be good on everything, from broiled fish and lamb chops to cooked beets, potatoes, asparagus, or green beans. Because the *romesco* pepper is difficult to find outside of Spain, ancho chiles are used here. Or, you can substitute 1 tablespoon ancho chili powder for the 2 ancho chiles, adding it to the blender or processor when you add the rest of the ingredients.

Here, I have called for a mixture of almonds and hazelnuts, but you can use one or the other. The recipe doubles or triples with ease—for a large summer party or for holiday gifts—and will keep in a tightly covered container in the refrigerator for up to 6 weeks.

MAKES ABOUT
2½
CUPS

2 ancho chiles
2 red bell peppers
½ cup hazelnuts
½ cup blanched almonds
4 cloves garlic, chopped
1 slice bread, fried in olive oil until golden and crisp and torn into pieces (optional)
1½ tablespoons sweet paprika or sweet smoked paprika
½ teaspoon hot paprika or hot smoked paprika
2 tablespoons tomato paste
¼ cup red wine vinegar
¾ cup extra virgin olive oil
Salt

1 Remove the stems and seeds from the ancho chiles and discard. Place the chiles in a small saucepan with water to cover, bring to a boil, remove from the heat, and let steep for 30 minutes. (You may need to weight down the chiles with a small plate to keep them submerged.)

2 Roast the bell peppers over the flame of a gas burner, turning as needed, until blistered and charred on all sides (or roast in a broiler). Transfer to a bowl, cover, and let rest for 20 minutes.

3 Preheat the oven to 350°F. Spread the hazelnuts on a small rimmed baking sheet and toast in the oven, stirring occasionally, until they are fragrant and their color deepens, about 10 minutes. Wrap the still-warm nuts in a dish towel and rub vigorously until most of the skins are removed (tiny flecks are okay), and then let cool. Toast the almonds on a separate baking sheet until fragrant and golden, about 8 minutes. Pour onto a plate to cool.

4 Drain the chiles, tear into small pieces, and place in a small bowl. Peel
the roasted peppers with your fingers, scraping off any stubborn pieces with
a paring knife (a few flakes clinging to the peppers are okay), and discard the
seeds and thick membranes. Cut the peppers into medium-sized pieces. Add
to the ancho chiles.

5 In a blender or food processor, combine the hazelnuts, almonds, garlic, and
bread, if using, and pulse until finely ground. Add the chiles and peppers, sweet
and hot paprika, tomato paste, and vinegar and process to combine. With the
machine running, slowly pour in the olive oil and process until the mixture emul-
sifies. Season to taste with salt and then adjust with more vinegar and/or hot
paprika if needed.

6 Transfer to a tightly covered container and refrigerate until needed. Bring to
room temperature before serving.

SAMFAINA

MIXED-VEGETABLE SAUCE

Samfaina, a classic of the Catalan kitchen and reminiscent of ratatouille, is a chunky blend of onions, garlic, eggplant, peppers, tomatoes, and zucchini, cooked down to a fragrant and unctuous stewlike sauce. The exact proportions are not crucial; a bit more tomato, a bit less bell pepper will not throw the sauce off. Some cooks add herbs at the end, and some add sweet paprika near the beginning. Neither is essential. The sauce makes a wonderful addition to a *tortilla* (use 2 cups well-drained sauce for 6 or 8 eggs), or it can be served hot or warm alongside grilled fish, used as braising sauce for chicken, or used as a topping for a COCA (page 69). For a simple tapa, spread it on grilled bread.

Japanese eggplants are easy to work with and hold their shape well, but a globe eggplant can also be used. Salting the eggplant before cooking means that it will absorb less oil when it is fried. The recipe yields about 8 cups. You can cut the recipe in half if you can find a small eggplant or use Japanese eggplants.

The sauce will keep in a tightly covered container in the refrigerator for up to 5 days. Bring it to room temperature or rewarm slightly before serving.

MAKES ABOUT

8

CUPS

1 pound Japanese eggplants, or 1 globe eggplant, about 1 pound

Salt

½ cup extra virgin olive oil

2 large onions, cut into ½-inch dice

4 to 6 cloves garlic, minced

1 teaspoon sweet paprika (optional)

½ pound zucchini, cut into ½-inch dice (about 2 cups)

2 small green or red bell peppers, seeded and cut into ½-inch dice (about 2 cups)

1½ pounds tomatoes, peeled, seeded, and cut into ½-inch dice (2½ to 3 cups)

2 tablespoons chopped fresh flat-leaf parsley (optional)

1 teaspoon chopped fresh thyme (optional)

1 bay leaf (optional)

½ teaspoon freshly ground black pepper

1   If using Japanese eggplants, trim but do not peel and cut into 1-inch pieces. If using a globe eggplant, trim, peel, and cut into 1-inch cubes. Sprinkle the eggplant pieces with salt on all sides and place in a colander set in the sink. Leave to sweat and drain for 20 to 30 minutes, then pat dry with paper towels.

2   In a large sauté pan, heat the oil over medium heat. Add the onions and cook, stirring occasionally, until softened and translucent, 8 to 10 minutes. Add the garlic and paprika, if using, and cook, stirring occasionally, until fragrant, 1 to 2 minutes. Add the eggplants, zucchini, and bell peppers and cook, stirring often, for 5 minutes longer. Add the tomatoes, and, if using, the parsley, thyme, and bay leaf. Cover, and reduce the heat to low. Simmer gently until the vegetables are tender and the mixture is thickened and similar in texture to chunky applesauce, about 25 minutes.

3   Season the sauce with 2 teaspoons salt and the pepper. Taste and adjust with more paprika, if you like. Serve warm or at room temperature.

MOJO VERDE Y MOJO COLORADO

GREEN SAUCE AND RED SAUCE

The word *mojo* comes from *mojar*, "to wet" or "to dunk." It lends its name to these wonderful sauces from the Canary Islands. They are excellent spooned on fish, shellfish, chicken, vegetables, and PATATAS ARRUGADAS (page 76). Some recipes for *mojo verde* add a small amount of chopped green bell pepper or chopped fresh cilantro.

You can make these sauces a few hours ahead of time and leave them at room temperature to allow the flavors develop. Leftover sauce can be refrigerated for up to 1 day. Bring back to room temperature before serving.

**EACH RECIPE
MAKES ABOUT
1¼
CUPS**

MOJO VERDE: In a bowl, combine the parsley, garlic, salt, and cumin. Whisk in the oil and vinegar, and then whisk in the water (to mellow the vinegar). Let stand for 30 minutes to allow the flavors to develop before serving. Leftover sauce can be refrigerated, but the herbs will turn a sad brownish yellow, so try to use the sauce the same day you make it.

MOJO COLORADO: In a food processor, combine the garlic and bread crumbs and process until a smooth paste forms. Add the paprika, salt, and cumin and pulse to combine. Transfer to a bowl and whisk in the oil and vinegar. Then whisk in water as needed to thin so sauce can be easily drizzled.

Mojo Verde

1 cup chopped fresh flat-leaf parsley or part parsley and part cilantro

8 cloves garlic, minced

1 teaspoon salt

1 teaspoon cumin seeds, toasted in a dry pan until fragrant, and finely ground

½ cup extra virgin olive oil

3 to 4 tablespoons white wine vinegar

2 tablespoons water

Mojo Colorado

10 cloves garlic, chopped

¼ cup fresh bread crumbs from day-old white bread

1 tablespoon hot paprika

½ teaspoon salt

1 teaspoon cumin seeds, toasted in a dry pan until fragrant, and finely ground

¾ cup extra virgin olive oil

¼ cup red wine vinegar

2 to 4 tablespoons water

The key word here is *shop*. Buy only the best ingredients, and you won't go wrong (see The Spanish Pantry, page 21, for information on unusual ingredients and their sources). Have on hand a few nice platters, some small *cazuelas* and attractive plates, a variety of little bowls for dipping sauces, toothpicks, and cocktail napkins, and you are set to serve.

Many of these tapas are put together with no cooking, with only a simple assembly of ingredients needed. Some require minimal cooking, such as a short time under the broiler, in the toaster oven, on a griddle, on the grill, in a sauté pan, or immersed in hot oil. All of the dishes are wonderfully casual, fast, and easy, so few precise measurements or temperatures are included. You will find everything from stuffed eggs, marinated olives, and *montaditos* to *banderillas* and *fritos* here. Use your imagination and have some fun. Just remember to taste before you serve.

SHOP-AND-SERVE TAPAS

ALMENDRAS FRITAS

FRIED MARCONA ALMONDS

Marcona almonds, which are grown along Spain's Mediterranean coast, are rounder, richer, and sweeter than the typical American almond. They can be purchased fried and salted or blanched. If you have purchased the former, just warm them in a dry pan or in a tablespoon or two of olive oil over low heat for a few minutes, shaking the pan from time to time, and serve them warm. Or, you can serve them straight from the jar or bag at room temperature.

If you have purchased blanched almonds, pour olive oil to a depth of 1 inch into a deep frying pan and heat over medium heat until hot. To test if the oil is ready, drop in 1 almond; it should sizzle. Add the almonds, a handful at a time, and fry until golden and crisp, about 5 minutes. Using a slotted spoon, transfer to paper towels to drain briefly, and then sprinkle with coarse sea salt (and with a pinch of cayenne pepper or hot paprika if you like) and serve warm. Alternatively, toast the blanched almonds in a 350°F oven, stirring occasionally, until golden brown, about 10 minutes, season with sea salt and pepper or paprika, and serve warm.

ACEITUNAS ALIÑADAS

MARINATED OLIVES

Marinate the olives for at least 2 days before serving. They will keep well for up to 1 week in the refrigerator and should be brought to room temperature before serving. Or, they are more flavorful—and sexier—if you warm them slightly, either in a frying pan for a few minutes over low heat or in a microwave oven for 30 seconds.

Combine 1 pound brine- or oil-cured black olives with 3 garlic cloves, crushed; 1 teaspoon each ground cumin and red pepper flakes; about ½ cup olive oil, or as needed to cover. Toss well, cover, and refrigerate.

Rinse the brine from 1 pound brine-cured green olives. Add 4 cloves garlic, crushed; 1 tablespoon dried oregano; 4 narrow orange or lemon zest strips; ¼ cup fresh orange or lemon juice; and ½ cup olive oil, or as needed to cover. Toss well, cover, and refrigerate.

HUEVOS RELLENOS

STUFFED EGGS

I suggest using the smallest eggs you can find because they are easier to pick up and eat in one or two bites and jumbo eggs are too rich and filling. Place the eggs in a saucepan with cold water to cover. Bring to a boil over high heat, reduce the heat to low, and cook at a gentle simmer for 9 to 10 minutes. Drain and rinse under running cold water. When they are cold, peel, cut in half lengthwise, and scoop the yolks into a bowl.

For 12 egg yolks, add 6 tablespoons mayonnaise, 2 teaspoons Dijon mustard, and salt, freshly ground black pepper, and some chopped fresh flat-leaf parsley to taste to the yolks and mix well. Spoon the stuffing into the egg halves, and top each stuffed egg with a thin strip of serrano ham or a sliver of smoked salmon, if desired. Garnish with a sprinkle of sweet paprika or sweet smoked paprika. Or, make the stuffing as directed and fold in one of the following: 3-ounce can or jar olive oil–packed tuna, drained and mashed; ¼ pound cooked peeled shrimp, chopped; ¼ pound fresh-cooked crabmeat, flaked; or 1 to 2 tablespoons each chopped capers and gherkins. Spoon the stuffing into the egg halves and garnish with sweet paprika or sweet smoked paprika.

GARBANZOS

CHICKPEAS

In a bowl, combine 1 can (15 ounces) chickpeas, drained and rinsed; 6 *piquillo* peppers, seeded and chopped; and ¼ pound dry chorizo, cut into ½-inch pieces. Add 4 to 6 tablespoons minced red onion and 1 clove minced garlic, and toss well. Dress with extra virgin olive oil and a little sherry vinegar, coating lightly. Serve at room temperature, or heat in a microwave oven for 1 to 1½ minutes and serve warm. Accompany with country bread.

In a bowl, combine 1 can (15 ounces) chickpeas, drained and rinsed; ½ cup finely minced red onion, 1 can or jar (about 7½ ounces) olive oil–packed tuna, drained; 3 tablespoons chopped fresh flat-leaf parsley; and 4 to 6 tablespoons chopped *piquillo* peppers. Dress lightly with extra virgin olive oil and fresh lemon juice or red wine vinegar. Accompany with country bread.

PIMIENTOS

PEPPERS

I buy small green *padrón* peppers, a specialty of Galicia, at my local farmers' market. (Shishito peppers, small green peppers sold in Japanese markets, are similar and can be prepared the same way.) Occasionally, one of these peppers will surprise you with a jolt of fire, but in general they are mild. Fry them in olive oil over high heat for just a few minutes, and then drain on paper towels and sprinkle with coarse salt. Serve hot.

Preserved whole *piquillo* peppers are a versatile staple of the tapas menu. To make *piquillos aliñados* (marinated *piquillo* peppers), drain 1 jar (8 ounces) of the peppers, cut into wide strips, and place in a bowl. Add 1 clove garlic, sliced paper-thin; 1 tablespoon sherry vinegar; 2 tablespoons extra virgin olive oil; and a little chopped fresh flat-leaf parsley and toss to mix. Serve as is, or top with strips of anchovies (*boquerones*).

To make *piquillos rellenos* (stuffed *piquillo* peppers), drain well, pat dry, and carefully remove the seeds. Stuff with one of the following combinations:

- Mashed canned or jarred olive oil–packed tuna mixed with mayonnaise to bind and seasoned with a little minced red onion, grated lemon zest, or tapenade and salt and freshly ground black pepper.

- Flaked fresh-cooked crabmeat or cooked baby shrimp mixed with mayonnaise to bind and a little chopped celery or green onion; drizzle with olive oil.

- Flaked fresh-cooked crabmeat mixed with softened cream cheese to bind, a little chopped celery, and fresh lemon juice to taste.

- Softened fresh herbed goat cheese; warm stuffed peppers gently in a 325°F oven for 10 to 15 minutes.

- Softened fresh goat cheese and ricotta cheese, with or without toasted pine nuts and plumped golden raisins; warm stuffed peppers gently in a 350°F oven for 10 minutes and drizzle with extra virgin olive oil and *moscatel* vinegar.

MARISCOS

SEAFOOD

Purchase anchovies (*boquerones*), arrange on a plate, and accompany with toasted country bread; place atop sliced tomatoes and onions, and drizzle with olive oil; or layer with strips of *piquillo* pepper and drizzle with olive oil.

Shave or grate *huevas de atún* or other salted fish roe over potato salad, sliced tomatoes, or scrambled eggs. Or, cook scrambled eggs with chives, top with shaved salted roe, and tuck into small soft rolls to make sandwiches (*bocadillos*).

Thinly slice *mojama* (air-dried tuna loin) just before serving and drizzle with olive oil. Or, serve with a tomato salad or over *piquillo* peppers or a bean salad.

Serve olive oil–packed canned tuna or homemade tuna confit atop a bed of sliced *piquillo* peppers or with tomato or potato salad. Or, mash canned tuna with mayonnaise to bind, season with a little minced red onion or grated lemon zest, and tuck into small soft rolls to make sandwiches, or spoon atop toasted or grilled country bread.

Combine 2 hard-boiled eggs, chopped; ¼ pound peeled cooked shrimp, chopped; 2 tablespoons grated carrot; and 1 lettuce leaf, finely shredded, with mayonnaise seasoned with ketchup (*salsa rosa*) to bind and tuck into hollowed-out small rolls to make open sandwiches (*bocadillos abiertos*).

Smoked salmon is not traditionally Spanish, but it is sometimes seen in tapas bars. Serve rolled around chunks of herbed cheese or tucked into small, soft buttered rolls to make sandwiches.

CHORIZOS, JAMÓN SERRANO Y LOMO CURADO

SAUSAGES, SERRANO HAM, AND CURED PORK LOIN

- Thinly slice dry chorizo and serve on a plate.

- Stuff pitted dates with strips of dry chorizo.

- Cut semicured chorizo into chunks, heat in red wine, and serve warm with toothpicks.

- Cut semicured chorizo into chunks, thread onto skewers alternately with shrimp, and cook on a grill.

- Cut semicured chorizo into chunks, thread onto skewers alternately with mushroom caps and strips of roasted pepper, and cook under the broiler.

- To make *chorizo a la sidra* (chorizo cooked in cider), a specialty of Asturias, cut ½ pound semicured chorizo into ½-inch-thick slices. In a sauté pan, heat 2 tablespoons olive oil over medium heat. Add the chorizo slices and 2 Golden Delicious apples, peeled, quartered, and cored (optional). Sauté until lightly colored on both sides. Add 1 cup hard cider, raise the heat, and bring to a boil. Reduce the heat to low and simmer, uncovered, until the chorizo is tender and the cider has reduced by half, about 8 minutes. Transfer to a bowl and serve with bread for dunking.

- Slice *serrano* ham or cured pork loin and arrange on a plate or atop grilled country bread. Serve alongside slices of melon, fig, mango, or other fruit.

- Slice *serrano* ham or cured pork loin and tuck into small buttered rolls, with or without cheese, for sandwiches (*bocadillos*).

- In a sauté pan, sauté ½ pound wild mushrooms, sliced; ¼ cup slivered *serrano* ham; and 1 clove garlic, minced, in 2 tablespoons olive oil or unsalted butter until the mushrooms are tender. Add 4 eggs lightly beaten with 1 tablespoon milk, and cook until soft curds form. Spoon into small rolls for sandwiches.

- Wrap a slice of *serrano* ham around a watermelon cube, pierce with a toothpick, and drizzle with olive oil. Add a cube of goat cheese to the skewer.

- Wrap a slice of *serrano* ham around a slice of melon, fig, peach, mango, Fuyu persimmon, or pear and pierce with a toothpick.

- Cut figs in half lengthwise, lay a fresh mint leaf wrap on each half, wrap with a slice of *serrano* ham, and brush lightly with extra virgin olive oil. Grill or broil until the ham is slightly crispy at the edges. Serve hot or warm, if possible, or at room temperature.

- Wrap *serrano* ham around crisp-cooked asparagus spears and serve warm or at room temperature with SALSA ROMESCO (page 32) or ALIOLI (page 30) for dipping.

- Top a slice of *serrano* ham with a slice of a good melting cheese, such as young Manchego, Monterey Jack, or Swiss and then with 2 parboiled asparagus spears. Roll up, dip in egg and then in flour, and sauté in olive oil until golden.

- Wrap a slice of *serrano* ham around a shrimp and sear on the grill; serve with a lemon wedge.

MONTADITOS

TAPAS SERVED ON BREAD

Montaditos, also known as *tostas*, are foods spread on toasted bread. The bread must be crusty, flavorful, and hearty; the olive oil fruity; the garlic pungent but not bitter; and the grill or broiler hot enough to mark the bread evenly. Cut the bread into slices about ½ inch thick, brush both sides with olive oil, and grill or broil until marked on both sides and somewhat crisp. Immediately rub the toasted bread on one side with a garlic clove and top with one of the following:

- To make *pa am tomàquet* (tomato-rubbed grilled bread), a popular Catalan tapa, rub the cut side of a ripe tomato half on the still-hot garlic-rubbed bread and sprinkle with salt and freshly ground black pepper. If desired, garnish with an anchovy (*boqueron*) fillet or a slice of *serrano* ham.

- Spread olive purée or tapenade on toasted bread and top with thin slices of smoked trout or smoked cod.

- Spread olive purée on toasted bread and top with a slice of *piquillo* pepper and an anchovy fillet.

- Spread olive purée on toasted bread and top with a layer of *requesón* or ricotta cheese and slivers of *piquillo* pepper.

- Spread olive purée thinned with mayonnaise on toasted bread and top with a piece of smoked trout.

- Spread puréed *piquillo* peppers on toasted bread and top with an anchovy fillet.

- Spread toasted bread with ALIOLI (page 30) or plain mayonnaise, and top with small cooked shrimp or pickled seafood (mussels, small octopus, or anchovies).

- Combine chopped hard-boiled eggs, anchovies, black olives, and capers with a little mayonnaise or olive oil and spread on toasted bread.

- Combine flaked fresh-cooked crabmeat or cooked baby shrimp with mayonnaise to bind, season with chopped green onion and grated lemon zest, and spread on toasted bread.

- Mix Cabrales cheese with enough milk or cream to make it spreadable, and fold in chopped toasted walnuts, if desired. Spread on toasted bread, top with pear or apple slices, and garnish with minced chives.

- Mash olive oil–packed tuna with mayonnaise or olive oil to bind, season with chopped capers, minced garlic, and fresh lemon juice, and spread on toasted bread.

- Mash canned sardines with mayonnaise to bind, spread on toasted bread, and top with chopped hard-boiled eggs.

- Top toasted bread with a slice of *serrano* ham and crown with a fried quail egg; garnish with strips of roasted pepper.

- Top toasted bread with a slice of *serrano* ham and a slice of *torta del Casar* or Brie cheese; melt under the broiler.

- Scramble eggs with strips of *piquillo* pepper and chopped anchovies, and spread on toasted bread.

- Mix crushed canned chickpeas with extra virgin olive oil, fresh lemon juice, and a bit of minced garlic. Add a bit of chopped fresh flat-leaf parsley, a generous sprinkle of hot paprika or hot smoked paprika, and pile on toasted bread. Top with strips of *piquillo* pepper.

BANDERILLAS

FOODS SPEARED ON TOOTHPICKS

- Wrap an anchovy (*boqueron*) fillet around a strip of *piquillo* pepper and spear with a toothpick.

- For the Gilda *banderilla*, named for the Rita Hayworth movie, spear an anchovy, caper berry or green olive, and a pickled *guindilla* chile (a specialty of the Basque kitchen) or other small pickled chile on a toothpick.

- Spear a slice of cooked potato or hard-boiled egg and a slice of tomato on a toothpick. Serve with ALIOLI (page 30) for dipping.

- Spear a rolled slice of smoked salmon, a slice of cooked potato, and a green olive or caper berry on a toothpick.

- Spear a piece of smoked trout, a smoked mussel, or a cooked shrimp; a cube of avocado; and a sliver of red onion on a toothpick.

- Spear a piece of chorizo and a cube of Manchego cheese on a toothpick.

- Spear of a piece of chorizo and a cube of melon or apple on a toothpick.

- Sprinkle a cube of watermelon with hot paprika or hot smoked paprika, wrap in a strip of *serrano* ham, and spear on a toothpick with or without a cube of fresh goat cheese. Drizzle with extra virgin olive oil and top with chopped fresh mint.

- Wrap a jumbo shrimp in *serrano* ham and sear on a grill or a stove-top grill pan until the ham takes on a bit of color. Sprinkle with freshly ground black pepper, spear on a toothpick, and serve with ALIOLI (page 30), SALSA ROMESCO (page 32), or lemon wedges.

- Slice Manchego cheese into ¼-inch-thick triangles, leaving the black rind intact. Slice quince (*membrillo*) into logs about 2 inches long and 1½ inches wide, and place a log atop each cheese triangle, centering it. Secure together with a toothpick and serve with bread or crackers.

FRITOS

FRIED FOODS

Deep-fried foods are quick and easy to make. The batter goes together with just a few strokes of the whisk, and once the oil is hot, the frying takes only a few minutes.

To make the batter, in a bowl, whisk together 1 cup all-purpose flour, ½ teaspoon baking powder, and ½ teaspoon salt. Add 2 large eggs, lightly beaten, and about 1 cup very cold water or sparkling water. It should be the consistency of heavy cream.

To deep-fry, pour canola or peanut oil to a depth of about 3 inches into a deep saucepan and heat to 360°F on a deep-frying thermometer, or until a cube of bread dropped into the oil turns golden brown within about 1 minute. Working in batches to avoid crowding, dip the foods into the batter, allowing the excess batter to drip off, and lower carefully into the oil. Fry until golden, turning gently in the oil, if needed, to cook evenly. Using a slotted spoon, transfer to paper towels to drain briefly and serve right away.

Some options for frying:

- Cut eggplant into batons 2½ inches long and 1 inch wide and thick. Sprinkle with salt and place in a colander in the sink to sweat and drain for 20 to 30 minutes. Then pat dry with paper towels. Dip in batter, fry, and drain as directed. Sprinkle with sea salt and drizzle with a little honey, if you like.

- Cut zucchini, bell peppers, and mushrooms into 1-inch pieces or into batons 2½ inches long and ¾ inch wide and thick. Dip in batter, fry, and drain as directed. Sprinkle with sea salt and serve with ALIOLI (page 30), SALSA ROMESCO (page 32), or lemon wedges.

- Cut cauliflower into 1-inch florets. Or, trim off the prickly tops and remove the leaves from small artichokes until you reach the tender pale green leaves; then trim off the stem and any dark green areas on the base, cut in half lengthwise, and trim away the choke. Parboil the cauliflower florets or artichokes in boiling water until crisp-tender, drain, and pat dry. Dip in batter, fry, and drain as directed. Sprinkle with sea salt and serve with ALIOLI (page 30), SALSA ROMESCO (page 32), or lemon wedges.

- Cut 1 pound firm, meaty white fish fillet into 1-inch cubes. Or, peel and devein medium shrimp; cut cleaned squid bodies into 1-inch-wide rings and leave the tentacles whole, or cut in half if large; or steam open and shell clams or mussels. For added flavor, marinate the fish, shrimp, or squid before frying. In a small bowl, stir together 2 tablespoons white wine vinegar or fresh lemon juice; 2 cloves garlic, minced; 2 teaspoons dried oregano; 2 teaspoons chopped fresh thyme; 1 teaspoon cumin seeds, toasted in a dry pan until fragrant and finely ground; 1 teaspoon sweet paprika; ¼ cup extra virgin olive oil; and salt and freshly ground black pepper. Rub the marinade on the fish cubes, shrimp, or squid, coating well, cover, and marinate at room temperature for up to 1 hour or in the refrigerator for up to 4 hours. Dip in batter (or dust with all-purpose flour, tapping off the excess), fry, and drain as directed. Sprinkle with sea salt and serve with ALIOLI (page 30), SALSA ROMESCO (page 32), or lemon wedges.

- For simple eggplant sandwiches, cut a globe eggplant lengthwise into thin slices. Place a slice of a good melting cheese, such as young Manchego or Gruyère, on half of the eggplant slices and top with the remaining eggplant slices. Pour canola oil (or part olive oil and part canola oil) to a depth of 1 inch into a large sauté pan and heat over medium-high heat. Dip the eggplant sandwiches first into beaten egg and then into flour and fry, turning once, until golden on both sides, about 3 minutes on each side. Drain briefly on paper towels and serve warm.

- For *queso frito* (fried cheese), remove the black rind from a ½-pound piece of Manchego cheese and cut into 6 wedges each ½ inch thick. In a bowl, stir together 1 cup fresh bread crumbs and 2 teaspoons chopped fresh thyme. In a second bowl, beat 1 large egg until blended. Pour canola oil (or part olive oil and part canola oil) to a depth of ¼ inch into a large sauté pan and heat over high heat. Dip the cheese wedges first in the egg and then in the bread crumbs and fry, turning once, until golden on both sides, about 30 seconds on each side. Drain briefly on paper towels and serve warm with SALSA ROMESCO (page 32) for dipping, if desired.

EGGS, FRITTERS, AND SAVORY PASTRIES

While Spaniards seldom eat eggs for breakfast, they do commonly eat them at tapas bars in a variety of guises, including stuffed; in *tortillas* (omelets); and *revueltos*, softly scrambled and served on toasted bread or tucked into a small roll for a *bocadillo* (sandwich) (see Shop-and-Serve Tapas). They are also cracked atop vegetable or meat and vegetable *cazuelas* (casseroles) and cooked until set on the stove top or in the oven, or they are hard boiled, chopped, and mixed with preserved fish or olives and capers for spreading on toasted bread.

Eggs are equally indispensable in the making of fritters and croquettes, an assortment—shrimp, ham and cheese, salt cod, potato—of which appear in the following pages. These deep-fried tapas are particularly popular in southern Spain, where frying is an art, as a visit to one of the famed *freidurias*, or fried fish shops, of Cádiz, in Andalusia, illustrates.

In this chapter, you will also find the filled pastries that have been prepared in Spain since medieval times, when they were a vital part of both Moorish and Sephardic kitchen traditions. *Empanadillas* are little pies—usually half-moons—that are fried or baked, while empanadas (once called *tapadas*, from *tapar*, or "to cover") are large double-crusted baked pies. The *cocas* of Majorca, which are a bit like pizzas, turn up here, too, topped simply with onions or greens and enjoyed along with a glass of the local wine.

TORTILLA ESPAÑOLA

POTATO AND ONION OMELET

Most of us are acquainted with the Mexican tortilla, a griddle-cooked corn-flour or wheat-flour pancake. But in Spain, a *tortilla* is a firm omelet, much like an Italian frittata. Traditionally, it is cooked in a generous amount of olive oil in a well-seasoned cast-iron skillet, but I have found that a nonstick pan is a good alternative. Here, I have used a 10-inch pan, but you can use an 8-inch pan and reduce the ingredient amounts proportionately to make a smaller omelet that will yield 4 servings.

This potato and onion *tortilla*, commonly thought to have originated in Castile, and a tapas bar classic, is sometimes made with potatoes only, or with the addition of a little chorizo or ham and/or peppers. But many other types are also made, from mushroom to caramelized onion to SAMFAINA (page 34). Typically, the *tortillas* are cut into wedges or squares and served at room temperature. At the popular Cal Pep, one of best tapas bars in Barcelona, the *tortilla* arrives with a layer of ALIOLI (page 30) spread on top. At other bars, *alioli* is sometimes served on the side.

Traditional recipes call for starting with sliced raw potatoes and cooking them in a generous amount of olive oil. To save time—and for a slightly less oily *tortilla*—you can parboil the potatoes until they are cooked through but still firm and then fry them in just half the amount of oil called for in the recipe. Russets have relatively soft pulp, so they will absorb more oil and will have a more tender texture. Yukon Golds, which are firmer, tend to hold their shape better. The russets are sliced before parboiling, but the Yukon Golds can be parboiled whole and then sliced. In either case, be careful not to overcook the potatoes. They should be cooked through but still firm.

CONTINUED

SERVES
6–8

About 1 cup extra virgin olive oil

1 pound russet or Yukon Gold potatoes, peeled and sliced ¼ inch thick

Salt and freshly ground black pepper

1 onion, thinly sliced

6 large eggs

2 or 3 ounces *serrano* ham or dry chorizo, diced (optional)

4 whole *piquillo* peppers or 1 large roasted red bell pepper, seeded and diced (optional)

Chopped fresh flat-leaf parsley for garnish

1   In a 10-inch frying pan, heat the oil over medium heat. Add half of the potato slices and fry, turning once or twice, until tender yet still firm and not browned, 10 to 15 minutes. Don't worry if they stick to one another a little. Using a slotted spatula, transfer to a platter and season with salt and pepper. Add the remaining potato slices to the pan, cook them the same way, and transfer them to the platter and season with salt and pepper. Pour out the oil and reserve. Set the pan aside.

2   In a smaller frying pan, heat about 2 tablespoons of the reserved oil over medium heat. Add the onion slices and cook, stirring from time to time, until soft and golden, 10 to 12 minutes. Transfer to a plate and let cool slightly.

3   In a large bowl, whisk the eggs until blended. Add the potatoes, onion, and 1 teaspoon salt and stir to distribute evenly. Fold in the ham and piquillos, if using.

4   Return the pan used for the potatoes to medium-high heat and add ¼ cup of the reserved oil. When the oil is hot, pour in the egg mixture. Let the eggs set without stirring, but shake the pan from time to time to make sure they are not sticking. After 3 to 4 minutes, cover the pan, reduce the heat to low, and cook until the bottom of the omelet is set and golden, the top edges are set, and the center is almost set, about 8 minutes.

5   Invert a large plate or lid on top of the frying pan, invert the plate and pan together, and lift off the pan. Add a bit more oil to the pan, and then slide the *tortilla*, browned-side up, back into the pan. Cook until the eggs are set on the bottom, 3 to 4 minutes longer. (Alternatively, omit flipping the omelet and instead finish cooking it in a preheated 400°F just until the top is set, about 8 minutes.)

6   Slide the omelet out onto a plate. Let it cool a bit and then sprinkle with the parsley. Cut into wedges and serve warm or at room temperature.

NOTE: You can cook the omelet in the oven, which is foolproof and stress free, though it will not be as creamy in the center. Preheat the oven to 350°F. Liberally oil a 7-by-11-by-2-inch baking dish (Pyrex is ideal) or an ovenproof 10-inch frying pan. Pour in the egg mixture and bake until the eggs are set and the top is lightly colored, 20 to 25 minutes. If you used a baking dish, run a knife around the inside edge of the dish to loosen the omelet and cut into squares to serve. If you used a sauté pan, run a knife around the inside edge of the pan to loosen the omelet, slide it out onto a plate, and cut into wedges to serve.

SPANISH: fino sherry JEREZ, Garnacha rosé NAVARRE
NON-SPANISH: Pinot Blanc CALIFORNIA, FRANCE,
                  dry rosé RHÔNE VALLEY, FRANCE; CALIFORNIA

TORTILLA DE AJOS TIERNOS SPRING GARLIC OMELET

Omit the potatoes and onion, and the peppers and ham, if desired. Sauté 8 green onions (including tender green tops), finely chopped, and ½ cup coarsely chopped green garlic or 2 to 3 cloves garlic, minced, in 2 tablespoons olive oil until tender. Let cool slightly, and add to the beaten eggs. Proceed as directed.

SPANISH: Viura RIOJA, fino sherry JEREZ
NON-SPANISH: Pinot Grigio ITALY, CALIFORNIA, Grüner Veltliner AUSTRIA

TORTILLA DE ESPÁRRAGOS TRIGUEROS ASPARAGUS OMELET

Omit the potatoes, onion, peppers, and ham. Trim off the tough ends from ¾ pound pencil-thin asparagus spears, cut into 1-inch pieces, blanch in boiling salted water, drain, and refresh in cold water. Sauté 3 spring onions or 8 green onions, thinly sliced, and 2 cloves garlic, thinly sliced, in 2 tablespoons olive oil until tender. Let cool slightly, and then add to the beaten eggs with the asparagus. Proceed as directed.

SPANISH: Verdejo RUEDA, fino sherry JEREZ
NON-SPANISH: Sauvignon Blanc FRANCE, AUSTRALIA, SOUTH AFRICA,
Pinot Blanc ITALY, FRANCE, CALIFORNIA

TORTILLA DE GAMBAS SHRIMP OMELET

Omit the potatoes, onion, peppers, and ham. Sauté 2 spring onions or 6 green onions, thinly sliced, in 2 tablespoons olive oil until tender. Let cool slightly, and then add to the beaten eggs with 1½ cup chopped cooked shrimp (about ½ pound). Proceed as directed. Chefs Diego Ruiz and Enrique Becerra in Seville turn a similar mixture that also includes asparagus into small savory flans, a modern refashioning of a classic tapa.

SPANISH: Chardonnay/blend CATALONIA, COSTERS DEL SEGRE, manzanilla sherry JEREZ
NON-SPANISH: Chardonnay OREGON, NEW ZEALAND, Vermentino ITALY

BASQUE OMELET

The difference between a *tortilla* and a *revuelto* is that the *tortilla* is firm and the *revuelto* is soft and creamy, as in this classic Basque dish. Here, the simple combination of eggs, peppers, onions, and tomatoes is wonderful served as is, or it can be tucked into soft rolls for easy sandwiches.

1 In a sauté pan, warm the oil over medium heat. Add the garlic, onion, and bell peppers and cook, stirring often, until soft but not brown, about 10 minutes. Add the ham, if using, and tomatoes and cook, stirring occasionally, until thickened, about 5 minutes. Add the eggs, reduce the heat to medium-low, and stir gently until softly set, 3 to 4 minutes.

2 Transfer immediately to a serving plate to prevent further cooking. Sprinkle with salt and pepper, and serve hot.

SPANISH: Hondarribi TXACOLINA, Mencía GALICIA
NON-SPANISH: Assyrtiko GREECE, Carménère CHILE

VARIATION

Prepare the pepper, onion, and tomato mixture as directed. Using 1 or 2 eggs per person carefully break them, one at a time, onto the surface of the mixture. Cover the pan and cook just until the whites are set and the yolks are still runny.

SERVES
4-6

¼ cup olive oil

2 cloves garlic, sliced

1 onion, chopped

1 green bell pepper, seeded and diced

1 red bell pepper, seeded and diced

3 to 4 tablespoons chopped *serrano* ham (optional)

2 large tomatoes, peeled, seeded, and diced

5 eggs, lightly beaten

Salt and freshly ground black pepper

CROQUETAS DE JAMÓN Y QUESO

HAM AND CHEESE CROQUETTES

At tapas bars all over Spain, locals are quick to try the house-made *croquetas*, often a signature dish of the chef. They are typically bite-sized morsels with a crunchy golden crust of eggs and bread crumbs enclosing a creamy filling dotted with pieces of chicken, ham, shellfish, spinach, or cheese. This recipe makes a large batch, ideal for a party. You can cut it in half, or you can make the full recipe, deep-fry some of the croquettes, and store the rest in the refrigerator for frying at another time. They will keep nicely for up to 3 days.

These croquettes can be served just as they are. Some cooks like to serve them with *alioli* for dipping. Because there is ham in the mixture, I prefer an *alioli* lightly sweetened with quince.

1 **TO MAKE THE CROQUETTE BASE**, in a saucepan, bring the milk just to a simmer over medium heat and remove from the heat. While the milk is heating, in another saucepan, melt the butter over low heat. Add the onion, if using, and cook, stirring often, until translucent, about 5 minutes. Add the flour, stir well to combine, and cook, stirring constantly, for a few minutes. A very thick, smooth paste will form. Gradually add the hot milk to the flour paste while stirring constantly. Then continue to cook, stirring constantly, until a very thick béchamel sauce forms, about 3 minutes. Season to taste with the nutmeg, salt, and pepper. Remove from the heat and fold in the cheese, ham, and parsley, if using. Taste and adjust the seasoning.

2 Oil a 9-inch square pan. Pour or spoon the croquette base into it and spread it out to cool. (I pat it down with my hands, but you can use a rubber spatula or the back of a spoon.) Cover with plastic wrap and refrigerate until well chilled, about 2 hours.

CONTINUED

Croquette Base

3 cups whole milk

½ cup (4 ounces) unsalted butter

½ cup minced onion (optional)

⅔ cup all-purpose flour

Freshly grated nutmeg

Salt and freshly ground black pepper

1½ cups finely diced full-flavored cheese such as Manchego, Mahón, or Gruyère (5 to 6 ounces)

½ cup (2 to 3 ounces) chopped *serrano* ham

2 tablespoons chopped fresh flat-leaf parsley or other herb of choice (optional)

About 1 cup all-purpose flour

2 large eggs

About 1 cup fine dried bread crumbs

Canola or peanut oil for deep-frying

3 **TO ASSEMBLE AND FRY THE CROQUETTES,** place 1 large or 2 small wire racks on a baking sheet, or line a baking sheet with parchment paper, and place on a work surface. Arrange 3 shallow bowls near the baking sheet. Put the 1 cup flour in the first bowl, lightly beat the eggs with 2 tablespoons water in the second bowl, and put the bread crumbs in the third bowl. Dip a tablespoon in cold water and scoop up some of the croquette mixture. With wet hands, roll it into a 1½-inch ball or into the traditional torpedo shape, about 2 inches long. Drop it into the flour, roll it around, and shake off the excess. Then dip it into the eggs, allowing the excess egg to drip off, and finally drop it into the bread crumbs, again rolling to coat and shaking off the excess crumbs. Set on the rack or lined pan. Repeat until all of the croquette mixture is used up. Refrigerate the croquettes until well chilled, about 2 hours.

4 Pour the oil to a depth of 3 inches into a deep, heavy saucepan and heat to 360°F on a deep-frying thermometer. Carefully slip a few croquettes into the hot oil and fry until golden, about 3 minutes. Using a wire skimmer or slotted spoon, transfer to an ovenproof platter lined with paper towels to drain, and keep batches of the croquettes warm in a low oven until all of the croquettes are fried.

5 Arrange the croquettes on a warmed platter and serve at once.

SPANISH: cava CATALONIA, rosé RIOJA, NAVARRE
NON-SPANISH: sparkling wine CHAMPAGNE AND LIMOUX, FRANCE, rosé ITALY

VARIATIONS

This basic croquette base can be flavored in other ways. Omit the ham and cheese and add 1 cup well-drained mashed olive oil–packed canned tuna; ½ pound cooked ham, chopped; 1½ cups chopped cooked shrimp (about ½ pound); 1½ cups chopped well-seasoned cooked chicken; or ½ cup chopped fresh herbs of choice.

NOTE: Some cooks like to cut out shapes, rather than roll the croquette base into balls or the traditional torpedoes. Line the pan with plastic wrap, allowing the edges to overhang the sides, spread the croquette base in the lined pan, and chill as directed. Invert the pan onto a work surface, lift off the pan, and peel away the plastic wrap. Cut the slab into rounds or other shapes with a cookie or biscuit cutter or a knife. Fry as directed.

POTATO CROQUETTES WITH PIQUILLOS AND ONION

The *picador* is the person who rides into the bullfight arena on horseback and stabs the bull in its neck with a lance, drawing the first blood and thus weakening the animal before the matador approaches with his cape and sword. I have been unable to find out how this recipe came to be named for this fixture of the bullring, but these croquettes are delicious nonetheless. You can use baked russets or boiled Yukon Golds with equally good results.

MAKES ABOUT

24

CROQUETTES

2 pounds russet or Yukon Gold
    potatoes

3 tablespoons olive oil

1 onion, minced

1 roasted red bell pepper or
    4 whole *piquillo* peppers,
    seeded and finely diced

Freshly grated nutmeg or ground
    mace

Salt and freshly ground black pepper

About ¾ cup all-purpose flour

2 large eggs

About ¾ cup fine dried bread
    crumbs

Vegetable or olive oil for deep-frying

ALIOLI (page 30)

1   If using russet potatoes, preheat the oven to 400°F. Pierce the potatoes in a few places with fork tines, place in the oven, and bake until tender when pierced with the fork, about 1 hour. Remove from the oven, let cool until they can be handled, and then peel and pass the warm potato pulp through a ricer into a bowl, or mash in a bowl with a potato masher.

If using Yukon Gold potatoes, peel and cut into 2-inch pieces and place in a saucepan with salted water to cover. Bring to a boil, reduce the heat to medium, and cook until tender, about 20 minutes. Drain and pass the warm potatoes through a ricer into a bowl, or mash in a bowl with a potato masher.

2   In a sauté pan, heat the oil over medium heat. Add the onion and cook, stirring occasionally, until softened and translucent, about 8 minutes. Add the bell pepper and heat through. Using a slotted spoon, transfer the onion and bell pepper to paper towels to drain briefly, and then fold into the potatoes. Season the potatoes to taste with nutmeg, salt, and pepper. Cover and refrigerate until chilled to make the mixture easier to shape.

3 To assemble and fry the croquettes, place 1 large or 2 small wire racks on a baking sheet, or line a baking sheet with parchment paper, and place on a work surface. Arrange 3 shallow bowls near the baking sheet. Put the flour in the first bowl, lightly beat the eggs with 2 tablespoons water in the second bowl, and put the bread crumbs in the third bowl. Dip a tablespoon in cold water and scoop up some of the croquette mixture. With wet hands, roll it into a 1-inch ball or 1½-inch oval. Drop it into the flour, roll it around, and shake off the excess. Then dip it into the eggs, allowing the excess egg to drip off, and finally drop it into the bread crumbs, again rolling to coat and shaking off the excess crumbs. Set on the rack or pan. Repeat until all of the mixture is used up. Refrigerate the croquettes until well chilled, about 2 hours.

4 Pour the oil to a depth of 3 inches into a deep, heavy saucepan and heat to 360°F on a deep-frying thermometer. Carefully slip a few croquettes into the hot oil and fry until golden, about 5 minutes. Using a wire skimmer or slotted spoon, transfer to an ovenproof platter lined with paper towels to drain, and keep warm in a low oven until all of the croquettes are fried.

5 Arrange the croquettes on a warmed platter and serve at once. Pass the *alioli* at the table.

SPANISH: cava CATALONIA, Godello VALDEORRAS
NON-SPANISH: sparkling wine CALIFORNIA, AUSTRALIA, Garganega ITALY

BUÑUELOS DE BACALAO

SALT COD FRITTERS

I am giving you two versions of this classic Spanish fritter, one shaped and one dropped. The first one calls for mixing together salt cod and potatoes and forming the mixture into balls or ovals with your hands. The second version adds the salt cod and potato mixture to a choux pastry, which is then dropped into the hot oil from a spoon. The latter has a creamier texture.

If you are not sure of the quality of the salt cod, cook it, select the whitest and most tender pieces, and discard the rest. If you have discarded quite a bit, you may not need all of the potatoes. Both fritters are usually served with ALIOLI (page 30).

EACH RECIPE SERVES

8

Shaped Fritters

1 pound salt cod fillet

1 cup each water and whole milk or 2 cups water, or as needed to cover

2 tablespoons olive oil, plus more if needed for processing cod

2 boiling potatoes, about 12 ounces total weight

1 small onion, minced

4 cloves garlic, finely minced

2 large eggs, lightly beaten

3 tablespoons chopped fresh flat-leaf parsley

1 tablespoon all-purpose flour

Pinch of hot paprika or cayenne pepper

Freshly ground black pepper

Milk, if needed

About 1 cup fine dried bread crumbs (optional)

Olive or vegetable oil for deep-frying

1   Place the cod in a bowl with cold water to cover and refrigerate for 36 to 48 hours (the thicker the piece, the longer it will take), changing the water 3 or 4 times. Drain.

2   In a saucepan, combine the cod with water-milk mixture to cover, bring to a gentle simmer over low heat, and cook until quite tender when pierced with a fork, 10 to 18 minutes.

3   Remove from the heat, drain well, and allow the cod to cool until you can handle it. Shred the fish, discarding any errant bones, skin, or tough pieces. Transfer to a processor and pulse until broken into tiny fragments and almost puréed, adding a little oil if needed to help soften the cod and keep it moving in the machine. Transfer the cod to a bowl, cover, and set aside at room temperature.

4   While the cod cools, in a saucepan, combine the potatoes with salted water to cover and boil until tender when pierced with a fork, 20 to 25 minutes. Drain, let cool, and then peel and pass through a ricer into a bowl, or mash in a bowl with a potato masher. Set aside.

5   In small sauté pan, heat the 2 tablespoons oil over medium-low heat. Add the onion and cook, stirring occasionally, until softened and translucent, 3 to 5 minutes. Add the garlic and cook, stirring occasionally, for 2 minutes. Remove from the heat.

6   Add the potatoes and the onion mixture to the cod and mix well. Add the eggs, parsley, and flour, and combine until evenly mixed. Season with the paprika and black pepper. The mixture should be the texture of mashed potatoes. If it is too stiff or dry, beat in a little milk.

7   If you have time, cover and chill the mixture to make shaping the fritters easier. To shape the fritters, dampen you hands and shape a spoonful of the cod mixture between your palms into a 1-inch ball. For a crunchier exterior, roll each ball in a shallow bowl of the bread crumbs, coating evenly and shaking off the excess.

8   Pour the frying oil to a depth of 3 inches into a deep, heavy saucepan and heat to 360° to 365°F on a deep-frying thermometer. Carefully slip a few fritters into the hot oil and fry until golden, 4 to 5 minutes. Using a wire skimmer or slotted spoon, transfer to an ovenproof platter lined with paper towels to drain, and keep warm in a low oven until all of the fritters are fried.

9   Arrange the fritters on a warmed platter and serve at once.

---

1   Soak, cook, and shred the salt cod as directed for the shaped fritters.

2   In a food processor, combine the shredded cod and garlic, and pulse until finely chopped. Transfer to a bowl.

3   In a small saucepan, combine the water and butter and bring to a boil over medium heat. Add the flour all at once and stir vigorously until the mixture forms a ball that pulls away from the sides of the pan, about 4 minutes. Remove from the heat and transfer to the bowl of a stand mixer fitted with the paddle attachment. On low speed, add the eggs, one at a time, beating well after each addition until incorporated. On medium speed, add the salt cod and parsley and mix well. Season with salt and pepper.

4   Heat the oil as directed for the shaped fritters. Working in small batches, drop the cod mixture by tablespoonfuls into the hot oil and fry until golden, about 3 minutes. Using a wire skimmer or slotted spoon, transfer to an ovenproof platter lined with paper towels to drain, and keep warm in a low oven until all of the fritters are fried.

5   Arrange the fritters on a warmed platter and serve at once.

Choux Fritters

1 pound salt cod fillet

2 cloves garlic, finely minced

1 cup water or ½ cup each water and whole milk

4 tablespoons unsalted butter

⅔ cup all-purpose flour

4 large eggs

2 tablespoons chopped fresh flat-leaf parsley

Salt and freshly ground black pepper

Olive or vegetable oil for deep frying

SPANISH: cava CATALONIA, Albariño GALICIA
NON-SPANISH: sparkling wine ALSACE OR LOIRE VALLEY, FRANCE, dry Riesling AUSTRALIA, FRANCE

SHRIMP FRITTERS

These crisp little pancakes are a specialty of the Andalusian city of Cádiz, where the tiny local shrimp are often added to the batter while still alive. Indeed, they are so small that their shells are imperceptible once they are fried. Sometimes a little chickpea flour is used along with the all-purpose flour, but you can use only all-purpose flour and still have lovely crisp fritters.

SERVES

4

1 In a bowl, combine the flour, onion, if using, parsley, chives, lemon zest, if using, salt, pepper, and paprika and stir to combine. Stir in just enough water to make a mixture with the consistency of heavy cream or pancake batter. Cover and let rest in the refrigerator for at least 1 hour or up to 3 hours. Just before frying, fold the shrimp into the batter.

2 Pour the oil to a depth of ½ inch into a deep frying pan and heat to 350°F on a deep-frying thermometer, or until the oil ripples in the pan and is hot but not smoking. Working in batches to avoid crowding, drop the batter by the tablespoon into the hot oil and press with a spatula to flatten to a cake about 2½ inches in diameter. Cook until crisp and golden on the first sides, 1 to 2 minutes. Turn and cook until crisp and golden on the second sides, 1 to 2 minutes longer. Using a slotted spatula, transfer to an ovenproof platter lined with paper towels to drain. These are best served in batches right out of the pan. If you prefer to serve them all at once, keep them warm in a low oven for as short a time as possible.

3 Arrange the fritters on a warmed platter and serve at once with the lemon wedges.

SPANISH: cava CATALONIA, Verdejo RUEDA, SEGOVIA
NON-SPANISH: sparkling wine AUSTRALIA, CALIFORNIA, Sauvignon Blanc NEW ZEALAND

½ cup all-purpose flour or ¼ cup each all-purpose flour and chickpea flour

¼ cup minced onion (optional)

2 tablespoons finely chopped fresh flat-leaf parsley

1 tablespoon minced fresh chives

Grated zest of 1 lemon (optional)

1 teaspoon salt

¼ teaspoon freshly ground black pepper

Pinch of hot paprika, hot smoked paprika, or cayenne pepper

About 1 cup water or sparkling water

½ pound small shrimp, peeled, deveined, and coarsely chopped

Olive oil for frying

Lemon wedges for serving

GALICIAN DOUBLE-CRUSTED PIE

There are countless variations on what gets tucked into this famous double-crusted pie from the northwestern region of Galicia. Some cooks use leftover cooked meat or poultry for the filling; others use fish or shellfish. The crust varies, too, with some cooks favoring a pastry similar to the one used for EMPANADILLAS (page 66; double the recipe), and others calling for a bread dough, like the one used for COCAS (page 69). A paella or pizza pan makes an ideal vessel for this pie. To make smaller empanadas, cut the dough recipe in half, cut out 4-inch rounds, put 2 tablespoons filling on each round, fold in half, seal the edges, and bake for 20 to 25 minutes.

SERVES

10–12

Dough

1 cup warm water

Pinch of saffron threads, warmed and crushed (optional)

1 package (2½ teaspoons) instant yeast

4 cups all-purpose flour

2 teaspoons salt

½ cup olive oil

Fish filling (recipe follows) or meat filling (page 65)

1 large egg, lightly beaten

1 **TO MAKE THE DOUGH,** pour the water into the bowl of a stand mixer, add the saffron, if using, and yeast, and let stand until bubbles start to rise, about 5 minutes. Fit the mixer with the dough hook. Gradually mix in the flour, salt, and oil and then knead on low speed until the dough is smooth and no longer sticky and leaves the sides of the bowl cleanly, 8 to 10 minutes. (Or, you can stir the ingredients together with a wooden spoon until a dough forms, and then knead by hand on a lightly floured work surface until smooth and no longer sticky.)

2 Shape the dough into a ball, transfer to a large oiled bowl, and turn the dough to oil it on all sides. Cover the bowl and leave the dough to rise in a warm place until almost doubled in size, 40 to 60 minutes.

3 While the dough is rising, make the fish or meat filling. Preheat the oven to 400°F. Oil a rimmed pizza pan, a paella pan about 14 inches in diameter, or a large rimmed baking sheet.

CONTINUED

4 To assemble the pie, transfer the dough to a lightly floured work surface and cut into 2 pieces, one slightly larger than the other. Roll out the larger piece into a round 14 to 15 inches in diameter and ½ inch thick. Drape it around the rolling pin and transfer it to the prepared pan. Fill as directed in the filling recipe. Roll out the remaining piece of dough about 14 inches in diameter and ½ inch thick, drape it over the rolling pin, and lay it over the filling. Press the edges together to seal. Brush the edges and sides with the beaten egg to make sure the pie is sealed. Then brush the top with the remaining egg. Cut a few steam vents in the top.

5 Bake until golden brown, 35 to 40 minutes. Let rest for at least 10 minutes before serving. Cut into wedges and serve warm or at room temperature.

FISH FILLING

1 In a frying pan, heat the oil over medium heat. Add the onions and cook, stirring occasionally, until softened and translucent, about 8 minutes. Add the tomatoes and simmer until the tomato juices have evaporated, about 10 minutes. Add the piquillos, parsley, and oregano and cook, stirring occasionally, for 10 minutes to blend the flavors. Remove from the heat, season to taste with salt and pepper, and let cool completely before using.

2 Preheat the oven and then roll out the dough and line the pan as directed. Spread the cooled onion-tomato mixture evenly over the dough, leaving a 1-inch border uncovered. Distribute the tuna, hard-boiled eggs, and olives evenly on top. Top with the second crust and bake as directed.

SPANISH: Albariño GALICIA
NON-SPANISH: Sauvignon Blanc CHILE

⅓ cup olive oil

2 large onions, chopped

3 cups peeled, seeded, and chopped tomatoes

¾ cup chopped *piquillo* peppers or jarred pimientos (about 14 whole peppers)

2 tablespoons chopped fresh flat-leaf parsley

1 teaspoon dried oregano

Salt and freshly ground black pepper

1 can or jar (about 7½ ounces) olive oil–packed tuna, drained and flaked, or 1 cup flaked cooked salt cod (about ½ pound before cooking)

2 hard-boiled eggs, peeled and coarsely chopped

¼ cup chopped black olives

MEAT FILLING

1 In a frying pan, heat the oil over medium heat. Add the onions and bell peppers and cook stirring occasionally, until the onions are softened and translucent and the peppers are softened, about 10 minutes. Remove from the heat, season to taste with salt and pepper, and let cool completely before using.

2 Preheat the oven and then roll out the dough and line the pan as directed. Scatter the chorizo, ham, and pork evenly over the dough, leaving a 1-inch border uncovered. Spread the onion-pepper mixture evenly over the meats, and top evenly with the eggs and then with the tomato slices. Top with the second crust and bake as directed.

SPANISH: Mencía GALICIA
NON-SPANISH: Merlot CHILE, SOUTHWEST FRANCE

½ cup olive oil or lard

2 onions, chopped

1 red bell pepper, seeded and chopped

1 green bell pepper, seeded and chopped

Salt and freshly ground black pepper

½ pound dry chorizo, diced

¼ pound *serrano* ham, diced

½ pound cooked boneless pork or veal, diced

3 hard-boiled eggs, chopped

1 large tomato, thinly sliced

EMPANADILLAS

LITTLE PIES WITH THREE FILLINGS

These small savory pastries are served in tapas bars all over Spain, with fillings that range from the spinach, ham, or tuna included here to chorizo, anchovy, chicken and peppers, meat, and more. Here, the pies are made with a short crust, but you can also use a yeast dough, such as the one for the double-crusted pie on page 63 (use half of the yeast dough recipe for each filling). The pastries are often deep-fried, but I have baked these for ease. You can assemble the pies a day or two in advance, refrigerate them, and then bake them just before serving.

MAKES
24
SMALL PIES

1 TO MAKE THE DOUGH, put the flour in a bowl, make a well in the center, and add the oil, shortening, milk, baking soda, and salt to the well. Using a wooden spoon, gradually work the wet ingredients into the flour, mixing until the dough comes away from the sides of the bowl. Turn the dough out onto a lightly floured work surface and knead briefly until it comes together, then shape into a ball, cover, and let rest at room temperature for 20 to 30 minutes.

2 Make the spinach, ham, or tuna filling. Preheat the oven to 350°F. Lightly oil a large baking sheet.

3 On a lightly floured work surface, roll out the dough into a large, thin round (⅛ inch thick or less). Cut out 3-inch rounds. Place 1 tablespoon of the filling on the center of each round, dampen the edge, fold over, and seal the edge, either with the tines of a fork or by pinching it with your fingers to make a narrow rim. Arrange the filled pastries on the prepared baking sheet, and brush with the egg.

4 Bake the pastries until golden, 20 to 30 minutes. Remove from the oven and serve warm or at room temperature.

Dough

2 cups all-purpose flour

¼ cup olive oil

2 tablespoons solid vegetable shortening or lard

¼ cup whole milk, water, or beer

½ teaspoon baking soda

1 teaspoon salt

Spinach, ham, or tuna filling (facing page)

1 large egg, lightly beaten

SPINACH FILLING

In a sauté pan, heat the oil over low heat. Add the garlic and cook, stirring occasionally, until softened, 2 to 3 minutes. Add the tomatoes, raise the heat to medium, and simmer until the tomato juices have evaporated, about 10 minutes. Add the spinach, mix well, and cook, stirring occasionally, until the spinach is tender, 3 to 5 minutes. Remove from the heat, fold in the cheese, if using, pine nuts, and eggs, and season to taste with salt and pepper. Let cool completely before using.

SPANISH: fino sherry JEREZ, Cariñena CATALONIA, NAVARRE
NON-SPANISH: Grüner Veltliner AUSTRIA, Carignan SOUTHERN FRANCE, CALIFORNIA

⅓ cup olive oil

4 cloves garlic, minced

1½ cups peeled, seeded, and chopped tomatoes (about 3 large)

1½ pounds spinach, tough stems removed, rinsed, and chopped

5 ounces soft white cheese such as ricotta, *requesón*, or *fromage blanc* (optional)

½ cup pine nuts, toasted

2 hard-boiled eggs, peeled and coarsely chopped

Salt and freshly ground black pepper

HAM FILLING

In a sauté pan, heat the oil over medium heat. Add the onions and cook, stirring occasionally, until soft and pale gold, about 15 minutes. Add the tomatoes and garlic and cook, stirring occasionally, until the tomato juices have evaporated, 5 to 8 minutes. Add the ham and cook for 2 to 3 minutes longer. Remove from the heat, fold in the eggs, and season to taste with salt and pepper. Let cool completely before using.

SPANISH: Treixadura/blend GALICIA, Moristel SOMONTANO
NON-SPANISH: Viognier CALIFORNIA, AUSTRALIA, Pinot Noir OREGON, NEW ZEALAND

3 tablespoons olive oil

2 onions, chopped

2 tomatoes, peeled, seeded, and chopped

2 cloves garlic, minced

2 thick slices cooked ham (about 4 ounces), diced

2 hard-boiled eggs, peeled and coarsely chopped

Salt and freshly ground black pepper

TUNA FILLING

In a sauté pan, heat the oil over medium heat. Add the onions and cook, stirring occasionally, until soft and pale gold, about 15 minutes. Add the tomatoes and cook, stirring occasionally, until the tomato juices have evaporated, 5 to 8 minutes. Remove from the heat, fold in the tuna and eggs, and season to taste with salt and pepper. Let cool completely before using.

SPANISH: Viura Rioja, TARRAGONA, rosé UTIEL-REQUENA, VALENCIA
NON-SPANISH: Pinot Grigio ITALY, dry rosé CALIFORNIA, FRANCE

¼ cup olive oil

2 onions, chopped

2 tomatoes, peeled, seeded, and chopped

1 can or jar (about 7½ ounces) olive oil–packed tuna, drained and flaked

2 hard-boiled eggs, peeled and chopped

Salt and freshly ground black pepper

COCAS

MAJORCAN FLAT BREAD WITH TWO TOPPINGS

Coca, the popular flat bread of the Balearic Islands and Catalonia, comes in a variety of shapes—rectangle, square, oval, round—and with countless toppings, such as caramelized onions and anchovy, greens seasoned with ham, or SAMFAINA (page 34) and small dollops of fresh cheese. The dough varies, too, with some cooks preferring a modified pizza dough and others choosing a bread dough. I like to make a sponge first, to give the yeast a headstart and because it yields a lighter crust. In the past, this dough was made with lard, but nowadays olive oil is more common.

Cocas are usually served warm, not piping hot, though they are delicious even at room temperature.

1 TO MAKE THE DOUGH, first make a sponge. In the bowl of a stand mixer, sprinkle the yeast over the warm water. Add ¼ cup of the flour and stir to combine. Cover with plastic wrap and let stand at room temperature for about 30 minutes.

2 Add the remaining 3¼ cups flour and the cool water, oil, and salt to the sponge. Fit the mixer with the dough hook and mix on low speed until the dough is smooth and no longer sticky and leaves the sides of the bowl cleanly, about 10 minutes. (Or, you can stir the ingredients together with a wooden spoon until a dough forms, and then knead by hand on a lightly floured work surface until smooth and no longer sticky.)

3 Shape the dough into a ball, transfer to a large oiled bowl, and turn the dough to oil it on all sides. Cover the bowl and leave the dough to rise in a warm place until almost doubled in size, about 1 hour.

4 Turn the dough out onto a lightly floured work surface, punch it down, and shape into a ball, or divide in half and shape into 2 balls. Place on a floured baking sheet, cover, and let rest in the refrigerator for 30 minutes while you make the topping.

CONTINUED

MAKES

1

(11-BY-17-INCH) OVAL OR
2 (9-INCH) ROUNDS

Dough

1 tablespoon active dry yeast

¼ cup warm water

3½ cups unbleached all-purpose flour

¾ cup cool water

2 tablespoons olive oil

2 teaspoons salt

Caramelized onion topping (recipe follows) or mixed-greens topping (page 71)

Cornmeal for dusting (optional)

5 Ready the caramelized onion or mixed-greens topping. If you are using a baking stone, place it on the oven floor (being careful not to cover any heat vents) or on the lowest rack in the oven. Preheat the oven to 475° or 500°F (allowing at least 30 minutes if using a stone). If you are not using a stone, oil a large rimmed baking sheet.

6 Remove the dough from the refrigerator and place on a lightly floured work surface. Using your hands, gently press, lift, and stretch the dough into the desired shape and size: an 11-by-17-inch oval if making 1 flat bread, or a 9-inch round if making 2 flat breads. With your fingertips, form a slightly raised rim around the edge. (You can also roll out the dough with a rolling pin and then form the raised rim.) Transfer the dough to a floured (or cornmeal-dusted) baker's peel or rimless baking sheet, top with the selected topping, and slide the dough onto the hot stone. Or, shape the flat bread(s) on the oiled baking sheet, top with the selected topping, and place the pan on the lowest rack in the oven.

7 Bake until the edges of the crust are golden, 12 to 15 minutes. Cut into wedges and serve warm.

CARAMELIZED ONION TOPPING

¼ cup olive oil

8 cups sliced onions (about 6 onions)

2 tablespoons chopped fresh thyme or rosemary

2 tablespoons honey (optional)

6 salt-packed anchovies, rinsed, filleted, and each fillet cut in half lengthwise

Freshly ground black pepper

¼ cup pine nuts, toasted

¼ cup raisins, plumped in hot water and drained (optional)

1 In a large frying pan, heat the oil over medium heat. Add the onions and cook, stirring often, until golden and reduced in volume by almost half, about 30 minutes. Add the thyme and honey, if using, and cook, stirring often, for about 10 minutes longer to blend the flavors. Remove from the heat and let cool completely before using.

2 Spread the cooled onions on the prepared crust. Top with the anchovies, and sprinkle with the pepper, pine nuts, and raisins, if using. Bake as directed.

SPANISH: Treixadura/blend GALICIA, Tempranillo/blend RIOJA
NON-SPANISH: Chenin Blanc FRANCE, SOUTH AFRICA, Dolcetto ITALY

MIXED-GREENS TOPPING

1   Remove the tough stems from the spinach. Trim off the white stalks and tough center ribs from the Swiss chard. You should have about 1 pound chard after trimming. Cut the spinach and chard leaves into narrow strips. Rinse well and drain but do not pat dry.

2   In a large frying pan, heat the oil over medium heat. Add the green onions and sauté until wilted, about 3 minutes. Add the chard and cook, stirring occasionally, until it begins to wilt, about 5 minutes. Then add the spinach and continue to cook, stirring occasionally, until the chard and spinach are wilted, 3 to 5 minutes longer. Remove from the heat, transfer to a fine-mesh sieve, and drain well, pressing on the greens with the back of a spoon. Transfer to a bowl and season to taste with salt and paprika. Let cool completely before using.

3   Spread the cooled greens on the prepared crust, and scatter the tomato over the top. Bake as directed.

SPANISH: Mencía BIERZO, Sauvignon Blanc/blend COSTERS DEL SEGRE, CASTILE AND LEÓN
NON-SPANISH: Cabernet Franc LOIRE VALLEY, FRANCE,
Sauvignon Blanc LOIRE VALLEY, FRANCE; CHILE

VARIATION

Omit the tomato and add 3 tablespoons of toasted pine nuts to the cooked greens. Top the greens with 1 cup *requesón*, ricotta, or other soft curd cheese in small dollops.

1 pound spinach

2 bunches Swiss chard

3 tablespoons olive oil

6 green onions, white and tender
    green parts, chopped

Salt

Sweet paprika

1 large tomato, peeled, seeded, and
    chopped

Most tapas bar menus draw heavily on the wealth of vegetables that fill Spanish markets. Many of the dishes are based on Old World natives, such as eggplants (which might be fried and dusted with sugar) in the style of the Moors, or grilled and mixed with onions and peppers in the popular Catalan dish known as *escalivada*. But just as many tapas showcase the bounty that arrived from the New World, such as the beloved potato, which turns up spicy hot in *patatas bravas*, wrinkled in *patatas arrugadas*, or paired with chorizo in *patatas a la riojana*.

Spanish cooks, in big cities and small villages alike, traditionally look to the seasons when deciding on which vegetable tapas to prepare. In the springtime in Andalusia, they might serve fava beans and artichokes partnered in a simple stew or wiry *trigueros* (wild asparagus) baked with eggs. *Calçots*, large green onions that are harvested in early spring, grilled over a charcoal fire, and served with a heady *salsa romesco*, are so prized they merit an annual festival. Come fall, menus typically feature such dishes as peppers stuffed with meat or salt cod, or cabbage leaves rolled around a filling of pork sausage, raisins, and pine nuts, dolma-like preparations that probably originated with the Persians and were adopted by the Moors.

Fortunately, many vegetable tapas—the same dishes are often first courses in a multicourse meal—are served warm or at room temperature, saving the cook from rushing about to keep them hot until they are eaten. And unlike what is found on many American tables, where crunchy, crisp vegetables are the custom, Spanish vegetables are almost always cooked to a tenderness that produces a greater depth of flavor.

VEGETABLES

"FIERCE" POTATOES

It is impossible to resist these spicy potatoes, a tapas bar favorite. I have eaten them the size of fat French fries, but in this recipe I have cut them into rustic 1-inch pieces. You can instead cut them into precise 1- or 1½-inch cubes. Here, I have included a spicy tomato sauce, which you can add to the potatoes or serve alongside for dipping. Or, you can serve the sauced potatoes with ALIOLI (page 30) for dipping. A similar dish calls for cooking the potatoes in boiling water (sometimes tinged with saffron) and then tossing them in a frying pan with oil infused with hot paprika until they are a stunning red.

SERVES
4

1 Pour the oil to a depth of about 1 inch into a deep frying pan and heat over medium heat until hot. Add the potatoes (they should be immersed in the oil; add more oil if needed to cover), reduce the heat to low, and cook until the potatoes are tender, about 20 minutes.

2 Raise the heat to medium and continue to cook until the potatoes are browned. Using a slotted spoon, transfer to a *cazuela* and keep warm.

3 Pour off all but 1 tablespoon oil from the pan and return the pan to low heat. Add the flour and paprika and stir over low heat for a few minutes until a smooth paste forms. Slowly pour in the broth while stirring constantly. Add the vinegar and pepper flakes and simmer for about 5 minutes to blend the flavors. Stir in the tomato sauce, and then taste and adjust the seasoning with salt. Some like the sauce very hot.

4 Pour the sauce over the potatoes and serve warm. Or, pour the sauce into a small ramekin, spear the potatoes with toothpicks, and serve the sauce alongside for dipping.

Olive oil for frying

1 pound potatoes such as red or white creamer, Bintje, Fingerling, or small Yukon Gold, cut into 1-inch pieces

1 tablespoon all-purpose flour

1 teaspoon sweet paprika

½ cup beef broth

2 tablespoons aged sherry vinegar

½ teaspoon red pepper flakes

6 tablespoons tomato sauce or purée

Salt

SPANISH: rosé CAMPO DE BORJA, CIGALES, Cariñena/blend PENEDÉS, TARRAGONA
NON-SPANISH: dry rosé CALIFORNIA, FRANCE, Gamay BEAUJOLAIS, FRANCE

PATATAS ARRUGADAS

WRINKLED POTATOES

This interesting technique for cooking potatoes comes from the Canary Islands. Originally the potatoes were cooked in seawater, but nowadays cooks boil them in regular water with a generous measure of sea salt. Then the potatoes are cooked in the dry pan, which creates the wrinkled salty crust that gives them their name.

SERVES

4

1 Put the potatoes in a heavy pan wide enough to hold them in a single layer. Add the salt and water just to cover. Bring to a boil over high heat, reduce the heat to low, cover partially, and cook until the potatoes are tender, 15 to 20 minutes.

2 Pour off the water from the pan and return the potatoes in the pan to the stove top over low heat. Cook, shaking the pan from time to time so the potatoes turn occasionally and don't scorch, until the potatoes are dry and the skins are wrinkled. This will take about 10 minutes.

3 Transfer to a serving dish and serve hot, with the sauce for dipping.

SPANISH: manzanilla sherry JEREZ, Viura/blend RIOJA, PENEDÉS, ZARAGOZA
NON-SPANISH: Alvarinho PORTUGAL, dry muscat FRANCE

1½ pounds small Yukon Gold or
    white potatoes
½ cup coarse sea salt

MOJO VERDE and/or **MOJO COLORADO**
    (page 35)

PATATAS A LA RIOJANA

POTATOES AND CHORIZO, RIOJA STYLE

This lovely *cazuela* of potatoes and chorizo is ideal for sharing. I use a semicured chorizo that produces a contrast in textures between the tender potatoes and the chewy sausage that is particularly interesting. Modern chefs typically cut everything into a uniform size, but you can opt for more rustic random cuts on both the chorizo and the potatoes. I have tasted a version of this recipe made without chorizo, but it lacks the great flavor the sausage imparts to the pan juices.

SERVES

4-6

1   In a large frying pan, heat the 3 tablespoons oil over medium heat. Add the potatoes and sauté until pale gold, 10 to 15 minutes. Using a slotted spoon, transfer to a large plate. Add the chorizo to the oil remaining in the pan and fry over medium heat, until golden, adding more oil if the chorizo begins to stick, about 5 minutes. Using the slotted spoon, transfer to the plate with the potatoes.

2   Add the onion to the oil and drippings in the pan and sauté over medium heat until golden, 12 to 15 minutes. Add the bell peppers, garlic, chile, if using, and paprika and cook, stirring occasionally, for 5 minutes longer to blend the flavors.

3   Return the sausage and potatoes to the pan and add the water. Cover and cook over low heat until the potatoes are tender, about 20 minutes. If the pan seems dry, add a bit more more water.

4   Remove from the heat, season with salt and pepper, and transfer to a *cazuela* or other dish for serving. Sprinkle with the parsley and serve warm.

SPANISH: Tempranillo/blend RIOJA, VALDEPEÑAS, NAVARRE,
            Garnacha/blend NAVARRE, CAMPO DE BORJA
NON-SPANISH: Barbera ITALY, Malbec ARGENTINA

3 tablespoons extra virgin olive oil, plus more as needed

1 pound russet potatoes (2 large), peeled and cut into 1-inch-thick slices or large dice

6 ounces chorizo, preferably semicured, cut into ½-inch-thick slices

1 small onion, chopped

2 red bell peppers or 1 red and 1 green, seeded and chopped

2 cloves garlic, minced

1 small fresh chile, seeded and minced (optional)

1 teaspoon sweet paprika or sweet smoked paprika

½ cup water or dry white wine, or as needed

Salt and freshly ground black pepper

Chopped fresh flat-leaf parsley for garnish

VARIATION

Just before removing from the heat, whisk 2 large eggs, lightly beaten, into the pan to thicken the juices.

ENSALADA DE PATATES

POTATO SALAD

Also known as *patatas aliñas*, this potato salad is usually served atop grilled or toasted bread, making it a perfect *pincho* for those who love double carbs. For a nice flavor contrast, top the salad with tuna.

1 In a saucepan, combine the potatoes with salted water to cover, bring to a boil, reduce the heat to medium, and cook just until tender when pierced with a knife, 20 to 25 minutes. Drain well, let the potatoes cool until they can be handled, and then cut into ½-inch dice.

2 In a bowl, combine the still-warm potatoes, the oil, and the vinegar and toss gently to coat evenly. Let cool completely and then fold in the mayonnaise, eggs, green onions, and olives. Season to taste with salt and pepper.

3 Spread the potato mixture on the bread slices, dividing it evenly. Top with the tuna and serve.

SPANISH: Hondarribi TXACOLINA, dry amontillado sherry JEREZ
NON-SPANISH: Tocai Friulano ITALY, Rousanne/blend RHÔNE VALLEY, FRANCE; CALIFORNIA

TUNA CONFIT

Preheat the oven to 250°F. Cut a 2-pound tuna fillet into 2-inch-thick pieces. Season the pieces with salt and pepper, and place in a single layer in a baking dish. Add 8 black peppercorns, bruised; 2 cloves garlic, crushed; 3 bay leaves; 1 teaspoon fennel seeds; and 1 lemon, thinly sliced. Pour in extra virgin olive oil to cover the tuna. Cover the dish with aluminum foil and bake until tender, 45 to 50 minutes. Remove from the oven and let cool completely. Pick through and discard the bay leaves, lemon slices, and garlic cloves, and then pack the tuna into a glass jar or plastic container. Strain the juices from the baking dish and pour over the tuna. Add extra virgin olive oil to cover. Cover tightly and refrigerate for up to 1 week. Bring to room temperature before serving.

SERVES

4

½ pound medium-sized white or Yukon Gold potatoes

1 tablespoon olive oil

2 tablespoons white wine vinegar, or to taste

¼ cup mayonnaise or **ALIOLI** (page 30)

2 hard-boiled eggs, peeled and chopped

4 green onions, including tender green tops, minced

¼ cup green olives, pitted and chopped

Salt and freshly ground black pepper

4 slices country bread, grilled or toasted

1 can or jar (about 7½ ounces) olive oil–packed tuna, drained and flaked, or Tuna Confit

CHAMPIÑONES AL AJILLO

GARLICKY FRIED MUSHROOMS

The term *al ajillo* is attached to dishes that call for frying foods—shrimp, squid, mussels, clams, chicken pieces, mushrooms—in olive oil with garlic and, sometimes, a bit of chile. These garlicky mushrooms can be served in a dish with bread on the side for sopping up the juices, or they can be spooned atop grilled or toasted bread and served as a *pincho*. You only use cultivated white mushrooms here, but combining white mushrooms with chanterelles and cremini will produce a tastier dish.

SERVES

4–8

1   In a large frying pan, heat the oil over high heat. Add the mushrooms and cook until golden on the undersides, about 3 minutes. Turn the mushrooms over and cook until the second sides are colored, 1 to 2 minutes longer.

2   Add the garlic and ham, if using, reduce the heat to medium, and cook for 1 minute. Add the wine and cook just until it has evaporated, about 2 minutes. Add the parsley, stir well, and season to taste with salt and pepper.

3   Serve at once, in a dish with the bread on the side or spooned atop the bread.

SPANISH: Godello VALDEORRAS, Monastrell JUMILLA, YECLA
NON-SPANISH: Chardonnay CHABLIS AND MACONNAIS, FRANCE, Xinomavro GREECE

6 tablespoons olive oil

1 pound cultivated white mushrooms, stem ends trimmed and halved if large

2 tablespoons minced garlic

¼ cup finely diced *serrano* ham (optional)

¼ cup dry white wine or dry fino or manzanilla sherry

¼ cup chopped fresh flat-leaf parsley

Salt and freshly ground black pepper

4 slices country bread, grilled or toasted

VARIATIONS

Add ½ cup toasted, skinned, and chopped hazelnuts with the parsley. Or, omit the ham and add ¼ pound chopped dry chorizo and ½ cup chopped toasted almonds with the garlic.

GRILLED EGGPLANT, ONIONS, AND PEPPERS

Grilling produces the characteristic smoky taste that is essential to a good *escalivada* (*escalivar* means "to cook in the ashes"). But you don't have to make a fire every time you crave this Catalan dish. Here, the onions and eggplants are roasted alongside each other, and the bell peppers and tomatoes are cooked over the flame of a gas stove. The finished dish is served at room temperature with bread on the side, spooned atop grilled or toasted bread, or layered with ham or chicken in sandwiches (*bocadillos*). For a contemporary presentation, cut all of the vegetables into ½-inch dice. For a more rustic presentation, follow the instructions here in the method. This dish releases liquid as it sits, so you may want to dress it—or refresh the dressing—at serving time. Some cooks top the finished dish with chopped fresh oregano along with the parsley, and with a few strips of anchovy or sardine fillet.

SERVES

8

2 onions, unpeeled

Extra virgin olive oil for rubbing, plus ½ cup

2 globe eggplants

2 red bell peppers

3 large tomatoes

¼ cup sherry vinegar or red wine vinegar

1 clove garlic, minced (optional)

Salt and freshly ground black pepper

¼ cup chopped fresh flat-leaf parsley

Chopped fresh oregano for garnish (optional)

Country bread for serving

1 Preheat the oven to 400°F.

2 Put the onions in a small baking pan and rub them with a little oil. Roast until tender when pierced with a knife, at least 1 hour. Remove from the oven, let cool until they can be handled, and then peel and slice ½ inch thick.

3 Prick the eggplants in several places with a fork, place them in a separate baking pan, and roast alongside the onions, turning them occasionally for even cooking, until soft but not mushy when pierced with a knife, about 45 minutes. Remove from the oven, let cool until they can be handled, and then peel the eggplants and tear the flesh into large strips, discarding any large seed pockets. Place in a colander to drain. (If you prefer a smoky flavor, omit the pricking step and broil the eggplants or cook them over medium heat on a stove-top cast-iron grill griddle, turning them often for even cooking.)

4   Roast the bell peppers over the flame of a gas burner, turning as needed, until blistered and charred on all sides (or roast in a broiler). Transfer to a bowl, cover, and let rest for 20 minutes. Peel the roasted peppers with your fingers, scraping off any stubborn pieces with a paring knife (a few flakes clinging to the peppers are okay), and discard the seeds and thick membranes. Cut or tear the peppers into strips about ½ inch wide.

5   Roast the tomatoes over the flame of a gas burner, turning as needed, until blistered and charred on all sides (or roast in a separate baking dish in the oven with the onions and eggplants for about 15 minutes). Scrape off the peel with a paring knife and cut or tear the tomatoes into strips or cut into dice.

6   Combine the onions, eggplants, roasted peppers, and tomatoes in a large bowl. In a small bowl, whisk together the ½ cup oil, vinegar, and garlic, if using. Season to taste with salt and pepper. Pour the dressing over the eggplant mixture and toss gently to coat. Taste and adjust the seasoning.

7   Transfer to a serving dish, sprinkle with the parsley, sprinkle with oregano, if using, and serve at room temperature. Serve the bread alongside.

SPANISH: Mencía BIERZO, GALICIA, Tempranillo/blend RIBERA DEL DUERO, TORO
NON-SPANISH: Petit Sirah aka Durif CALIFORNIA, AUSTRALIA, Zinfandel CALIFORNIA

ESPINACAS CON PASAS Y PIÑONES

SPINACH WITH RAISINS AND PINE NUTS

Any time you see raisins and pine nuts in a Spanish recipe, you can be sure its origins are Moorish. This dish is equally at home in Catalonia or Andalusia. Málaga is the home of Spain's most spectacular raisins, so it comes as no surprise that *acelgas a la malagueña*, Swiss chard prepared the same way, is popular there, though, in true Moorish tradition, without the ham. Although some recipes suggest boiling the spinach, it is unnecessary. Just wilt it in the rinsing water clinging to the leaves. Be sure to remove any tough stems, as they look stringy and unattractive after cooking. If the leaves are especially large, tear or cut them into smaller pieces for faster cooking and easier eating. A little chopped onion or minced *serrano* ham is occasionally added to the dish.

SERVES
4-6

1 In a bowl, combine the raisins with hot water to cover and set aside to plump for 30 minutes.

2 In a small, dry frying pan, toast the pine nuts over medium heat, shaking the pan often, until fragrant and golden, 3 to 5 minutes. Pour onto a plate to cool. (Alternatively, toast in a 350°F oven for about 8 minutes.) Or, if you prefer the flavor of sautéed pine nuts, heat 1 to 2 teaspoons oil in the frying pan over medium heat, add the nuts, sauté until golden and fragrant, and transfer to the plate with a slotted spoon to cool.

3 In a large sauté pan, heat 3 tablespoons oil over medium heat. Add the onion or ham, if using, and cook, stirring often, until the onion is softened and translucent or the ham is lightly colored, about 10 minutes for the onion and 5 minutes for the ham. Add the spinach with just the rinsing water clinging to its leaves and cook, turning and stirring constantly with tongs, until wilted, 3 to 5 minutes.

4 Drain the raisins and add to the pan along with the pine nuts. Stir well and season with salt and pepper. Transfer to a serving dish and serve warm.

¼ cup raisins

¼ cup pine nuts

3 tablespoons olive oil,
   plus 1 to 2 teaspoons for
   the nuts (optional)

1 small onion, chopped (optional), or
   3 ounces *serrano* ham, minced
   (optional)

2 pounds spinach, tough stems
   removed and rinsed

Salt and freshly ground black pepper

SPANISH: Verdejo RUEDA, Albariño/blend GALICIA
NON-SPANISH: Viognier CALIFORNIA, off-dry Riesling GERMANY, WASHINGTON

GARBANZOS CON ESPINACA

CHICKPEAS WITH SPINACH

Native to Iran, chickpeas were introduced to the eastern Mediterranean by the Greeks and Romans, but most scholars believe the Carthaginians carried chickpea seeds to Spain. Spinach arrived with the Moors. This classic pairing, from the kitchens of New Castile, began as a Lenten dish. In time, the combination was rounded out with the addition of salt cod and became an everyday dish, with the faithful sacrificing the salt cod during Lent. Today, the salt cod is sometimes replaced with a ham hock during the cooking of the beans and/or diced cooked ham to the finished dish. (If you opt to include the salt cod, be sure to omit the ham hock.) The stew is enriched with a *picada* of fried bread and garlic and is fairly thick and substantial. It may even be topped by fried or hard-boiled eggs.

SERVES

8

½ pound (1 generous cup) dried chickpeas

7 cloves garlic, peeled

1 onion, peeled

1 bay leaf

1 small ham hock (optional)

Salt

About 1¼ pounds spinach, tough stems removed, rinsed, and coarsely chopped (about 10 loosely packed cups or 1 pound after trimming)

2 tablespoons olive oil

1 slice country bread, crust removed

Generous pinch of saffron threads, warmed and crushed

1 teaspoon cumin seeds, toasted in a dry pan until fragrant and finely ground

2 teaspoons sweet smoked paprika

½ cup coarsely flaked cooked salt cod (optional)

¼ cup diced cooked ham if using ham hock or ½ cup if not using hock (optional)

Salt and freshly ground black pepper

Dash of sherry vinegar, as needed

4 eggs, fried sunny-side up, or 2 hard-boiled eggs, peeled and chopped (optional)

1 Pick over the chickpeas, discarding any misshapen peas or grit, rinse well, and soak overnight in water to cover. The next day, drain the chickpeas and put them in a saucepan with water to cover by 2 inches. Tie together 4 of the garlic cloves, the onion, and the bay leaf in a piece of cheesecloth and add the sachet to the pan. Add the optional ham hock only if you will not be adding salt cod later, and then bring to a boil over high heat. Reduce the heat to low and simmer uncovered, adding 2 teaspoons salt (less if using the ham hock) after the first 10 minutes of cooking, until the chickpeas are tender, about 1 hour. Remove the pan from the heat, and remove the sachet from the pan. Leave the chickpeas in their cooking liquid. Discard the ham bone. Untie the sachet, discard the bay leaf, and reserve the garlic and onion.

2 Place the spinach in a saucepan with only the rinsing water clinging to its leaves and cook over medium heat, stirring and turning constantly with tongs, until wilted, 5 to 6 minutes. Drain well in a sieve, pressing with the back of a spoon. If the leaves seem stringy or too big, you can chop them a bit more. Set aside.

CONTINUED

3 Heat the oil in a small sauté pan over medium-high heat. Add the bread and the remaining 3 uncooked garlic cloves and fry, turning as needed, until golden, 4 to 5 minutes. Transfer to a blender or small processor, add the saffron, and pulse until pulverized. Add the onion and garlic reserved from the chickpeas, the cumin, paprika, and 1 cup of the chickpea cooking liquid and purée until smooth.

4 Add the purée and the spinach to the cooked chickpeas along with the salt cod or the ham, whichever you are using. Place the mixture over low heat, stir well, and bring to a simmer. If it seems dry, add a little water as needed so the stew is spoonable. Season to taste with salt and lots of pepper. Taste and balance the seasoning with vinegar.

5 Transfer to a serving dish. If serving with the optional eggs, top with the fried eggs and serve hot, or with the hard-boiled eggs and serve warm.

SPANISH: rosé VALDEPEÑAS, CIGALES, Tempranillo/blend RIOJA, LA MANCHA, CATALONIA
NON-SPANISH: rosé of Pinot Noir FRANCE, CALIFORNIA, Cabernet/blend CHILE, ARGENTINA

CALÇOTS, ALCACHOFAS Y ESPÁRRAGOS CON ROMESCO

GRILLED GREEN ONIONS, ARTICHOKES, AND ASPARAGUS WITH SALSA ROMESCO

In early spring, when the large green onions called *calçots* appear in Barcelona's famed La Boqueria market, it's time to fire up the grill for the traditional *calçotada*, a feast that pairs the sweet, tender onions with *salsa romesco*. For this dish, buy spring onions, the largest green onions you can find, or baby leeks, though the latter are a bit more assertive in flavor. Traditionally, *calçots* are grilled two hours before serving. They are then wrapped in newspaper or plastic wrap to steam, so the burnt skin loosens and the insides become butter soft. To ensure tenderness, you will need to cook the onions thoroughly before grilling. For variety, and because they are in season at the same time, I like to grill some fat asparagus spears and artichokes to go along with the onions. The onions are quite juicy, so you might need to hand out bibs when everyone sits down to eat.

SERVES

8

1 lemon

4 artichokes

3 tablespoons olive oil

16 very fat spring or green onions or baby leeks, preferably about ¾ inch in diameter

16 large asparagus spears

Extra virgin olive oil for brushing

Salt and freshly ground black pepper

SALSA ROMESCO (page 32)

1   Fill a large bowl with cold water. Cut the lemon in half and squeeze the juice into the water. Working with 1 artichoke at a time, remove all of the tough, dark green outer leaves until you reach the pale green leaves. Cut off the prickly tops and trim off the end of the stem. Peel the stem and the dark green, tough outer layer from the base. Cut the artichoke in half, and scoop out the choke from each half with the tip of a spoon or a paring knife. Drop the halves into the lemon water to prevent discoloration.

2   When all of the artichokes are trimmed, bring a saucepan filled with salted water to a boil. Drain the artichokes, add them to the boiling water with the olive oil, and cook until just tender when pierced with a knife, about 20 minutes. Drain, immediately immerse in cold water to halt the cooking, and then drain again. Set aside.

CONTINUED

3   Soak 8 bamboo skewers in water to cover. Trim off the roots from the green onions and all but 4 inches of the green. Refill the saucepan with salted water, bring to a boil, add the onions, and cook at a simmer until the heads feel tender and crack slightly when you pinch them with your fingers, 8 to 10 minutes depending on their size. Do not undercook them because they will not soften much during grilling. Drain, immediately immerse in cold water to halt the cooking, and then drain again. Squeeze them dry. Drain 4 of the skewers and thread 4 onions on each skewer. Set aside.

4   Trim off the tough ends from the asparagus spears, and then, using a vegetable peeler, peel the bottom half of each spear. Refill the saucepan with salted water, bring to a boil, add the asparagus, and cook until crisp-tender, about 3 minutes. Drain, immediately immerse in cold water to halt the cooking, and then drain again. Drain the remaining 4 skewers and thread 4 asparagus spears on each skewer.

5   Prepare a fire in a charcoal or gas grill. Brush the artichokes, onions, and asparagus with the oil, and sprinkle with salt and pepper. Place over the fire and grill, turning as needed, until well browned and a little charred on all sides.

6   Transfer the vegetables to a platter, slipping them free of the skewers, and serve. Provide each guest with a bowl of the *romesco* for dipping.

SPANISH: Tempranillo/blend RIBERA DEL DUERO, TORO, Verdejo RUEDA, AVILA
NON-SPANISH: Syrah/blend RHÔNE VALLEY, FRANCE; WASHINGTON; CHILE, Muscadet FRANCE

CAZUELA DE ESPÁRRAGOS TRIGUEROS

ASPARAGUS, ANDALUSIAN STYLE

Each spring, the wild asparagus season is a much-anticipated event in Spain. The thin green stalks have a slight bitterness, unlike their sweeter cultivated kin. Look for cultivated pencil-thin asparagus to approximate the character of this Andalusian dish.

SERVES

4

1 Preheat the oven to 350°F.

2 Trim off the tough ends from the asparagus spears, then cut the stalks into 2-inch pieces. Bring a saucepan filled with salted water to a boil, add the asparagus, and cook until tender, about 3 minutes. Drain, reserving 2 cups of the cooking water, and set the asparagus and water aside separately.

3 To make a *picada*, in a frying pan, heat the oil over medium-high heat. Add the garlic and bread and fry, turning as needed, until golden, 4 to 5 minutes. Transfer the garlic and bread to a mortar, and set the pan aside. (Do not clean the pan. You want the garlicky oil to remain.) Add the saffron, paprika, peppercorns, and ½ teaspoon salt to the mortar and pound with a pestle until finely ground. Add 1 cup of the reserved cooking water and mix well. Or, combine the ingredients in a small processor or blender and pulse until finely ground, and then add the cooking water and process until mixed.

4 Return the pan with the garlic oil to medium heat, add the asparagus, and warm through. Add the *picada* and the vinegar, reduce the heat to low, and cook, stirring, for 3 to 4 minutes to coat the asparagus. If the mixture seems too dry, add a little of the remaining cooking water. Remove from the heat.

5 In a bowl, beat the eggs with 5 tablespoons water and a pinch of salt. Place 4 *cazuelitas* or ramekins on a rimmed baking sheet, and divide the asparagus evenly among the ramekins. Top with the egg mixture. Bake until the eggs are set, about 15 minutes. Remove from the oven and serve hot or warm.

1 pound pencil-thin asparagus spears

¼ cup olive oil

4 cloves garlic

2 slices country bread, crusts removed

¼ teaspoon saffron threads, warmed and crushed

1 teaspoon sweet paprika

8 black peppercorns

½ teaspoon salt, plus a pinch

2 tablespoons white wine vinegar

3 large eggs

SPANISH: fino sherry JEREZ, Mencía BIERZO; RIBEIRA SACRA, GALICIA
NON-SPANISH: Sauvignon Blanc SOUTH AFRICA, AUSTRALIA, NEW ZEALAND, Cabernet Franc FRANCE, CALIFORNIA

HABAS A LA GRANADINA

FAVAS WITH ARTICHOKES, GRANADA STYLE

This springtime vegetable stew from Andalusia has Moorish flavor notes of cumin, saffron, and mint. The tomato, however, is a New World touch. Some cooks garnish the dish with quartered hard-boiled eggs.

SERVES
4-6

1   Fill a large bowl with cold water. Cut the lemon in half and squeeze the juice into the water. Working with 1 artichoke at a time, remove all of the tough, dark green outer leaves until you reach the pale green leaves. Cut off all of the leaves at their base and then trim the stem flush with the base. Pare away the dark green, tough outer layer from the base. Cut the artichoke into quarters or eighths, and then scoop out the choke from each piece with the tip of a spoon or a paring knife. Drop the pieces into the lemon water to prevent discoloration.

2   Shell the fava beans. You should have about 3 cups. Bring a saucepan filled with salted water to a boil, add the fava beans, and boil for 2 minutes. Drain, immediately immerse in cold water, drain again, and peel away the tough outer skin from each bean.

3   In a large frying pan, warm the oil over medium heat. Add the onion and cook, stirring occasionally, until softened and translucent, 8 to 10 minutes. Add the garlic, cumin, and paprika and cook, stirring, for 2 minutes longer. Add the tomato and cook for 1 minute. Drain the artichokes and add to the pan along with the saffron infusion and water just to cover the vegetables. Add the bay leaf and the mint and parsley sprigs and simmer, uncovered, until the vegetables are tender, about 15 minutes. Add the favas during the last 3 minutes to heat them through. If there is too much liquid, raise the heat to high and cook until reduced.

4   Discard the bay leaf and parsley and mint sprigs. Stir in the shredded mint and chopped parsley and season to taste with salt and pepper. Transfer to a serving dish and serve warm.

SPANISH: fino sherry JEREZ, Mencía BIERZO; RIBEIRA SACRA, GALICIA
NON-SPANISH: Sauvignon Blanc SOUTH AFRICA, AUSTRALIA, NEW ZEALAND

1 lemon

4 artichokes

4 pounds young, tender fava beans

2 tablespoons extra virgin olive oil

1 small onion, chopped

2 or 3 cloves garlic, minced

1 teaspoon cumin seeds, toasted in a dry pan until fragrant and finely ground

1 teaspoon sweet paprika or sweet smoked paprika

1 tomato, peeled, seeded, and chopped

½ teaspoon saffron threads, crushed and steeped in 2 tablespoons boiling water

1 bay leaf

1 fresh mint sprig, plus 1 teaspoon finely shredded

2 fresh flat-leaf parsley sprigs, plus 2 tablespoons chopped

Salt and freshly ground black pepper

CHAMPIÑONES RELLEÑOS

SAUSAGE-STUFFED MUSHROOMS

The most common stuffing for this popular tapa mixes sausage or ham, onion, garlic, and the chopped stems from the mushrooms. The stuffed mushrooms are then topped with cheese, bread crumbs, or a mixture, and baked. Sautéing the mushroom caps in oil to soften them a bit before they are stuffed helps them to cook more evenly in the oven.

For this stuffing, I buy semicured chorizo, grind it in a food processor, and then sauté it with the onions and stems for a few minutes. If you can only find dry chorizo, chop it very finely in the processor and sauté it only briefly with the onion and stems to infuse the stuffing with its pronounced flavor. (If you can't find either type of chorizo, use ½ pound ground pork and season it with 2 teaspoons sweet smoked paprika, ½ teaspoon freshly ground black pepper, and 1 tablespoon minced garlic.) Any leftover filling is a great addition to scrambled eggs.

SERVES
6

12 large cultivated white mushrooms, about 2 inches in diameter

3 tablespoons olive oil

3 tablespoons unsalted butter

6 tablespoons finely minced onion

2 cloves garlic, finely minced

¼ cup minced *serrano* ham (optional)

¼ pound semicured chorizo, ground in a food processor

¼ cup toasted or fresh bread crumbs

2 tablespoons chopped fresh flat-leaf parsley, thyme, or marjoram

Salt and freshly ground black pepper

¼ cup grated Manchego cheese (optional)

1   Preheat the oven to 400°F. Carefully remove the stems from the mushrooms, and chop the stems finely. (You can do this in a processor, pulsing to chop.) You will need ½ to ⅔ cup chopped stems.

2   In a sauté pan, warm the oil over medium, high heat. Add the mushroom caps in batches and brown briefly on both sides, about 4 minutes total. Transfer to a *cazuela* or shallow baking dish, hollow-side up, and set aside.

3   Wipe out the sauté pan and melt the butter over medium heat. Add the onion and cook, stirring, until softened, about 5 minutes. Add the garlic and the stems and cook, stirring, until the stems are wilted, about 3 minutes. Add the ham, if using, and chorizo and cook, stirring, until the chorizo is cooked, about 3 minutes. Stir in the bread crumbs and parsley, and season to taste with salt and pepper, keeping in mind that the ham will give off more salt in the heat of the oven.

CONTINUED

4 Spoon the mixture into the mushroom caps, mounding it slightly. Sprinkle evenly with the cheese, if using. (The mushrooms can be prepared up to this point 4 to 8 hours in advance, covered, and refrigerated. Bring to room temperature before baking.)

5 Bake until the cheese is melted and the mushrooms are hot and bubbling about 15 minutes. Serve from the *cazuela* or transfer to a platter and serve hot or warm.

SPANISH: fino sherry JEREZ, Mencía BIERZO; RIBEIRA SACRA, GALICIA
NON-SPANISH: Sauvignon Blanc SOUTH AFRICA, AUSTRALIA, NEW ZEALAND,
Cabernet Franc FRANCE, CALIFORNIA

VARIATIONS

Add ¼ cup chopped toasted almonds to the stuffing with the parsley. Or, omit the cheese and add a pinch of ground cinnamon and 1 tablespoon grated orange zest with the chorizo.

LENTEJAS Y SETAS AL ESTILO DEL ALTO ARAGON

LENTILS AND MUSHROOMS FROM ARAGON

Look for small, dark lentils for this dish, such as brown *pardina* lentils from Spain, green lentils from France, or brownish green lentils from Umbria. During cooking, they hold their shape and texture better than red lentils or the average supermarket brown lentils, which are better for soup. The sautéed mushrooms and tomatoes give this dish a hearty profile. For additional flavor, add a little chopped *serrano* ham or cooked *morcilla* to the pan when you sauté the mushrooms.

SERVES

8

1   In a saucepan, combine the lentils with water to cover by 2 inches and bring to a boil over high heat. Reduce the heat to low and simmer gently, uncovered, 25 to 45 minutes, depending on the age of the lentils. Add 2 teaspoons salt after the first 10 minutes of cooking. Most of the liquid will have been absorbed by the lentils during cooking. If not, drain most of the liquid away, leaving a few tablespoons.

2   While the lentils are cooking, in a sauté pan, heat 3 to 4 tablespoons oil over medium heat. Add the onion, carrot, and fennel and cook, stirring occasionally, until tender, about 15 minutes. Add the tomatoes and garlic and cook, stirring occasionally, for a few minutes longer until the tomatoes have released some of their juices. When the lentils are ready, add the tomato mixture to them and toss to mix.

3   Rinse the sauté pan and heat ¼ cup oil over medium-high heat. Add the mushrooms and sauté until tender, about 5 minutes. Add the sherry and simmer for a minute or two to cook off some of the alcohol. Add the mushrooms to the lentils and toss to mix.

4   Season to taste with salt and pepper and transfer to a serving dish. Sprinkle with the mint and serve warm.

2 cups small green or brown lentils, rinsed

Salt

About ½ cup olive oil

1½ cups diced onion

½ cup diced carrot

½ cup diced fennel or celery

2 large tomatoes, peeled, seeded, and chopped

1 tablespoon minced garlic

6 to 8 ounces cultivated white or cremini mushrooms, stem ends trimmed and sliced ¼ inch thick

⅓ cup medium-dry sherry such as amontillado

Freshly ground black pepper

Finely shredded fresh mint for garnish

SPANISH: manzanilla sherry JEREZ, Monastrell ALICANTE, JUMILLA, YECLA
NON-SPANISH: Sangiovese/blend TUSCANY, Merlot SOUTHWEST FRANCE, SOUTH AFRICA

BERENJENAS RELLENAS A LA CATALANA

STUFFED EGGPLANTS, CATALAN STYLE

This Moorish-inspired recipe, with a flavor reminiscent of Greek moussaka, traditionally called for beef, but nowadays pork is more common. Some cooks spoon a light tomato sauce over the cooked eggplant.

SERVES
8–12

1 Preheat the oven to 350°F.

2 Trim away the stem end from each eggplant, and then cut in half lengthwise. With a sharp knife or a melon baller, remove the pulp, leaving a shell about ¼ inch thick. Set the pulp aside. Put the eggplant shells, hollow-sides up, in a single layer in a baking dish pan or *cazuela*, and brush them with the oil. Bake until soft when pierced with a knife, about 15 minutes. Remove from the oven and set aside. Alternatively, in a large sauté pan, heat 2 or 3 tablespoons of oil over medium heat. Add the eggplant shells and sauté, turning as needed, until softened, 8 to 10 minutes, and then set aside.

3 Chop the eggplant pulp coarsely. In a sauté pan, heat 3 tablespoons oil over medium-high heat. Add the beef and cook, stirring occasionally, until browned, 8 to 10 minutes. Add the onion, garlic, and eggplant pulp and sauté until the eggplant is almost tender, about 5 minutes, Stir in the cinnamon and wine and cook until all of the liquid has been absorbed, about 5 minutes. Remove from the heat.

4 In a small saucepan, heat 1 tablespoon oil over low heat. Add the flour and stir for a few minutes until well combined but not browned. Gradually stir in the milk, raise the heat to medium, and cook, stirring, until thickened, 3 to 4 minutes. Season to taste with nutmeg, salt, and pepper. Remove from the heat.

8 Japanese eggplants

Olive oil

½ pound ground beef or pork

1 onion, finely chopped

2 cloves garlic, minced

½ teaspoon ground cinnamon

¼ cup dry white wine

1 tablespoon all-purpose flour

⅓ cup whole milk

Freshly grated nutmeg

Salt and freshly ground black pepper

2 large eggs, beaten

½ cup fine dried bread crumbs

Tomato sauce for serving (optional)

5 If you baked the eggplant shells rather than sautéing them, oil the same baking dish. If not, oil a baking dish or *cazuela* that will hold the stuffed eggplant halves comfortably, and arrange the eggplant shells, hollow-sides up, in it. In a small bowl, lightly beat 1 of the eggs. Fold the egg and the white sauce into the eggplant mixture, mixing thoroughly, and then spoon the filling into the eggplant shells. Beat the remaining egg, and spoon it evenly over the tops of the stuffed eggplants. Sprinkle evenly with the bread crumbs.

6 Bake until golden brown on top, about 20 minutes. Spoon a little tomato sauce, if using, over each eggplant and serve warm.

SPANISH: Garnacha MONSANT, NAVARRE, Monastrell JUMILLA, YECLA
NON-SPANISH: Zinfandel CALIFORNIA, Syrah/blend FRANCE, CALIFORNIA, WASHINGTON

VARIATION

To make a vegetarian filling, prepare and prebake the eggplant shells and coarsely chop the pulp as directed. In a sauté pan, heat 3 tablespoons olive oil over medium heat. Add 1 onion, chopped, and sauté until tender, about 8 minutes. Add 3 cloves garlic, minced, and the chopped eggplant pulp and cook until the eggplant is almost tender, about 5 minutes. Add 1 cup peeled, seeded, and chopped tomato; 3 tablespoons pine nuts, toasted; 3 tablespoons raisins, plumped; and a pinch of ground cinnamon and simmer for 3 to 4 minutes to blend the flavors. Season to taste with salt and pepper. Remove from the heat and fold in some fresh bread crumbs if the mixture is very wet. Spoon into the eggplant shells, sprinkle lightly with grated Manchego cheese, and bake as directed.

ROLLITOS DE COL RELLENOS

CABBAGE ROLLS

In Catalonia, cooks make a dish known as *farcellets de col*, which calls for flouring and frying cabbage rolls until golden and then heating them in meat broth. Here, in a simpler preparation, pork-filled cabbage rolls are assembled and then braised in a broth flavored with tomatoes. This recipe makes a large batch, but you won't have trouble convincing your guests to eat them. Pass slices of crusty bread for scooping up the pan sauce.

SERVES

8–12

1   In a bowl, combine the pork, chorizos, onion, garlic, pine nuts, raisins, bread crumbs, egg, paprika, and 1 teaspoon each salt and pepper. Mix well and set aside.

2   Bring a large pot two-thirds full of water to a boil. Meanwhile, using a sharp knife, cut out the tough core of the cabbage(s). Salt the water lightly and slip the cabbage into the pot. When the water returns to a simmer, adjust the heat to maintain a gentle simmer and cook gently until the cabbage leaves soften, about 10 minutes. Lift the cabbage out of the water and drain it in a colander. If using 2 cabbages, repeat with the second cabbage. Remove only the outer large leaves from the head(s). You need about 16 leaves in all. Reserve the remaining cabbage for another use. You can finely shred some and add to the filling.

3   Spread out the cabbage leaves, inside facing upward, on a work surface. Place a few tablespoons of the filling on the center of a leaf, fold the top of the leaf over to cover it, fold in the sides, and then fold up the bottom, making a neat package. Secure closed with a toothpick. Repeat until all of the filling is used.

1 pound ground pork

½ pound semicured chorizos or *morcillas* sausages, casings removed and finely chopped, or chopped bacon

1 onion, chopped

3 cloves garlic, minced

¼ cup pine nuts, toasted

¼ cup raisins, plumped in hot water for 30 minutes and drained

1 cup fresh bread crumbs

1 large egg, lightly beaten

1 teaspoon sweet paprika

Salt and freshly ground black pepper

1 large or 2 medium green cabbages

Sauce

2 tablespoons olive oil

1 large onion, chopped

1 teaspoon sweet paprika

2 cups peeled, seeded, and chopped tomatoes

About 2 cups beef broth

4 **TO MAKE THE SAUCE**, in a large Dutch oven or other heavy pot, heat the olive oil over medium heat. Add the onion and cook, stirring occasionally, until softened and almost golden, about 10 minutes. Add the paprika and tomatoes and cook until the tomatoes give off some of their juices, about 5 minutes. Place the cabbage packages in the pot, toothpick-side up, pour in enough broth to cover, and bring to a gentle boil. Reduce the heat to low, cover, and simmer gently until aromatic, the pan sauce has reduced slightly, and the cabbage leaves are very tender, 1 to 1½ hours. (Alternatively, braise in a 350°F oven for the same amount of time.)

5 If you want to reduce the pan sauce further, use a slotted spoon to transfer the cabbage packages to a plate and cover them with aluminum foil to keep warm. Reduce the sauce over high heat until the desired consistency.

6 To serve, transfer the cabbage packages to warmed *cazuelitas* or ramekins, remove toothpicks, and ladle on the pan sauce. Serve warm.

SPANISH: Treixadura/blend GALICIA, amontillado sherry JEREZ
NON-SPANISH: Gewürztraminer ALSACE, NEW ZEALAND, CALIFORNIA,
         dry or off-dry Riesling GERMANY, AUSTRIA, WASHINGTON

PIMIENTOS RELLENOS A LA RIOJANA

MEAT-STUFFED PEPPERS, RIOJA STYLE

Many different kinds of sweet peppers are grown in Spain, but the *piquillo* is among the most highly prized. Small, triangular, and sweet with just a hint of heat, the best *piquillos* come from the Navarre region, where they are roasted over wood fires and packed into jars or cans. If you cannot find *piquillos*, you can use red bell peppers, but seek out the smallest ones available and cut away the thick interior ribs.

You can simply stuff these peppers and then warm them through in hot broth. Or, for a slightly more elaborate—and tastier—preparation, you can stuff them, coat them with egg and flour, fry them until golden, and then warm them in hot broth.

1 In a frying pan, heat the oil over medium heat. Add the onion and chopped bell pepper and cook, stirring occasionally, until the onion is softened and translucent, about 8 minutes. Add the beef and garlic, and cook slowly, breaking up any lumps with a wooden spoon or spatula, until the meat is cooked through, 10 to 15 minutes. Stir in the butter and flour and simmer for 3 to 5 minutes to bind the mixture. Remove from the heat and season to taste with salt and pepper.

2 Slit each piquillo along one side and remove the seeds. Using a small spoon, carefully stuff the peppers with the meat mixture. Skewer each pepper closed with a toothpick if you will not be frying them. If you will be frying them, let the filling cool before you stuff the peppers, and then pinch the peppers closed and refrigerate for a few hours or until firm.

CONTINUED

SERVES

8

2 tablespoons extra virgin olive oil

1 onion, finely chopped

1 small green bell pepper, finely chopped

¾ pound ground beef or 6 ounces each ground beef and ground pork

1 clove garlic, minced

4 tablespoons unsalted butter

¼ cup all-purpose flour

Salt and freshly ground black pepper

16 to 24 whole *piquillo* peppers or 8 fresh red pimiento or small bell peppers, roasted and peeled

(For Optional Frying)

Canola oil or part olive oil and part canola oil for deep-frying

2 large eggs

About ½ cup all-purpose flour

1½ to 2 cups beef broth

2 tablespoons chopped fresh flat-leaf parsley

3   For best results, fry the peppers about 1 hour or so ahead of time and then heat them in the broth just before serving. To fry the peppers, pour the oil to a depth of 1½ inches into a deep sauté pan and heat to 370°F on a deep-frying thermometer. While the oil is heating, lightly beat the eggs in a shallow bowl. Spread some flour for dusting in a second shallow bowl. When the oil is ready, dip a stuffed pepper into the beaten eggs, allowing the excess to drip off, and then into the flour, coating evenly and shaking off the excess. Slip the pepper into the hot oil and repeat with more peppers, being careful not to crowd the pan. Fry until golden, 3 to 4 minutes. Using a slotted spoon, transfer to paper towels to drain.

4   Arrange the peppers—fried or unfried—in a *cazuela* or wide pan large enough to hold all of them in a single layer. Pour the broth over the peppers, cover, and cook over low heat for 10 minutes, or until heated through. Or, heat in a preheated 400°F oven for 10 to 15 minutes.

5   Sprinkle the peppers with the parsley and serve warm.

SPANISH: rosé NAVARRE, CIGALES, CAMPO DE BORJA,
         Garnacha/blend NAVARRE, CATALYUD, CARIÑENA
NON-SPANISH: dry rosé ITALY, FRANCE, CALIFORNIA,
         Pinot Noir ARGENTINA, CALIFORNIA, OREGON, NEW ZEALAND

VARIATION

Omit the beef broth. In a frying pan, heat 2 tablespoons olive oil over medium heat. Add 1 small onion, chopped, and 2 cloves garlic, minced, and cook, stirring occasionally, until the onion is softened and translucent, about 8 minutes. Add ½ pound red bell peppers, roasted, peeled, seeded, and chopped, or 1 jar (8 ounces) whole *piquillos* or pimientos, drained and chopped, and ½ cup chicken broth and simmer for 10 minutes to blend the flavors. Remove from the heat, pour into a blender or food processor, and process until smooth. Season to taste with salt and freshly ground black pepper. Use in place of the beef broth.

PIMIENTOS RELLENOS DE BACALAO

SALT COD–STUFFED PEPPERS, BASQUE STYLE

A simple salt cod stuffing fills these iconic peppers from the Basque Country, which are bathed in a mild tomato sauce. You can substitute fresh cod or another mild white fish for the salt cod.

SERVES
8-16

1 Place the cod in a bowl with cold water to cover and refrigerate for 36 to 48 hours (the thicker the piece, the longer it will take), changing the water 3 or 4 times. Drain.

2 In a saucepan, combine the cod with water to cover. Place over low heat and very slowly bring to a simmer. Remove from the heat when the water begins to boil. Let the cod cool in the water, and then drain the cod and break it into small pieces with your fingers, discarding any errant bones, skin, or tough pieces. Set aside.

3 In a sauté pan, heat 2 tablespoons of the oil over medium heat. Add 1 onion and cook, stirring occasionally, until soft and pale gold, 10 to 12 minutes. Add the tomato sauce, paprika, 2 tablespoons of the parsley, and the 2 tablespoons flour and stir well. Add the wine and broth and bring to a boil. Reduce the heat to low and simmer, stirring often, until thickened, 5 to 8 minutes. Remove from the heat and set aside.

4 In another sauté pan, heat the remaining 2 tablespoons oil over medium heat. Add the remaining onion and the garlic and cook, stirring occasionally, until tender, about 8 minutes. Add the cod and then the milk-soaked bread crumbs and season with salt and pepper. Reduce the heat to low and cook gently, stirring from time to time, until well mixed and softened, about 5 minutes. Add the egg yolk and the remaining 2 tablespoons chopped parsley and remove from the heat. Let cool completely.

5 Slit each piquillo along one side and remove the seeds. Using a small spoon, carefully stuff the peppers with the cod mixture and pinch closed. Refrigerate for a few hours or until firm.

¾ pound salt cod fillet

4 tablespoons extra virgin olive oil

2 small onions, finely chopped

½ cup tomato sauce

1 tablespoon sweet paprika

4 tablespoons chopped fresh flat-leaf parsley

2 tablespoons all-purpose flour, plus about ½ cup for dusting

¼ cup dry white wine

¼ cup fish broth or water

2 cloves garlic, minced

½ cup fresh bread crumbs, soaked in milk to cover and squeezed dry

Salt and freshly ground black pepper

1 large egg yolk, lightly beaten

16 whole *piquillo* peppers or 8 fresh red pimiento or small bell peppers, roasted and peeled

Canola or part olive oil and part canola oil for deep-frying

1 large whole egg

CONTINUED

6 Pour the oil to a depth of 1½ inches into a deep sauté pan and heat to 370°F on a deep-frying thermometer. While the oil is heating, lightly beat the whole egg in a shallow bowl. Spread about ½ cup flour for dusting in a second shallow bowl.

7 When the oil is ready, dip a stuffed pepper into the beaten egg, allowing the excess to drip off, and then into the flour, coating evenly and shaking off the excess. Slip the pepper into the hot oil and repeat with more peppers, being careful not to crowd the pan. Fry until golden, 3 to 4 minutes. Using a slotted spoon, transfer to paper towels to drain.

8 Transfer the tomato sauce to a large frying pan over medium heat. Add the fried peppers in a single layer and simmer for 10 minutes to blend the flavors.

9 Transfer to a serving dish and serve hot, warm, or at room temperature.

SPANISH: Hondarribi TXACOLINA, cava CATALONIA
NON-SPANISH: Pinot Gris FRANCE, OREGON, dry sparkling wine FRANCE, CALIFORNIA

Seafood has a prominent role on many tapas bar menus, especially in coastal communities where local cooks rely on an amazing variety of shellfish and fish pulled from the Mediterranean and the Atlantic. The Basques prepare all manner of shrimp, spiny lobsters, and spider crabs, with squid cooked in their ink being a specialty of the region. Tiny freshwater eels, served sizzling in olive oil with garlic and chile—al pil-pil style—in cazuelitas, are another favorite of Basque tapas bar patrons. Galician fisherman are particularly renowned for providing shellfish—scallops, clams, mussels, shrimp, cockles—to restaurants all over Spain. Back home, scallops are common on tapas menus, served a la plancha, baked with serrano ham, onion, and white wine, and countless other ways.

Escabeches, which call for cooking fresh shellfish or fish and then preserving them in a mild vinegar and olive oil brine, are also frequently served in tapas bars. So, too, are simple grilled, fried, or braised fish, such as atún a la plancha (tuna cooked on a griddle) or merluza a la sidra (hake cooked with hard cider). Yet despite this wealth of fresh seafood, salt cod, the answer to the religious prohibition of meat consumption on Fridays and during Lent in the days when easy transport and refrigeration were impossible, reaches across all regional borders, turning up in such classic tapas as atascaburras, a simple spread of cod and potatoes, or bacalao a la viscaina.

Because Spain boasts a long coastline and two island clusters, the Balearics and the Canaries, it comes as no surprise that seafood-based tapas are nearly as popular inland as they are near the shore. Even though this is the largest chapter in the book, what you will find in the following pages is only a small sampling of the seafood offerings that Spaniards regularly enjoy at tapas bars. For more ideas, see Eggs, Fritters, and Savory Pastries and Shop-and-Serve Tapas.

SEAFOOD

SALPICÓN DE MARISCOS

SEAFOOD COCKTAIL

This lively seafood salad is served all over Andalusia. Prepare the vegetables first, then make the dressing, and finally cook the shellfish. Don't throw out those shrimp shells. Instead, use them to make a quick broth for cooking all of the shellfish for the salad, to intensify their flavors. To save a little time, buy already-cleaned squid; you will need ⅜ pound.

SERVES 8

1 In a small bowl, whisk together the oil, garlic, and vinegar for a dressing and set aside.

2 Bring a saucepan of water to a boil over high heat. Drop in the shrimp shells, reduce the heat to medium, and simmer for 20 minutes. Drain through a fine-mesh sieve and discard shells.

3 Meanwhile, clean the squid as directed on page 25. Cut the bodies into ½-inch-wide rings. Leave the tentacles whole if small or cut in half if large.

4 Return the shrimp broth to the saucepan and bring to a bubbling simmer over medium heat. Add the shrimp and cook until pink, about 4 minutes. Using a slotted spoon, transfer the shrimp to a bowl. Add the scallops to the simmering broth and cook until opaque, 2 to 3 minutes. Using the slotted spoon, add the scallops to the shrimp. Finally, add the squid to the simmering broth and cook just until opaque, about 1 minute. Using the slotted spoon, add the squid to the shrimp and scallops.

½ cup extra virgin olive oil

1 clove garlic, minced

3 tablespoons white wine vinegar or fresh lemon juice

½ pound shrimp, peeled and deveined, with shells reserved

1 pound squid (uncleaned weight), preferably small

½ pound scallops, tough side muscle removed

1 pound clams, scrubbed

1 red bell pepper, seeded and cut into ¼-inch dice

1 green bell pepper, seeded and cut into ¼-inch dice

1 small red onion, finely chopped

15 to 20 cherry tomatoes, stemmed and halved (optional)

3 tablespoons chopped fresh flat-leaf parsley

2 tablespoons salt-packed capers, well rinsed

3 gherkins, chopped (optional)

5 Pour off all but 1 cup of the broth from the pan. Bring the broth remaining in the pan to a boil over high heat. Add the clams, discarding any that are cracked, cover, and cook, shaking the pan occasionally, until the clams open, 3 to 6 minutes (some may be stubborn). Remove them as they open and keep steaming until they finally surrender. When cool enough to handle, remove the meats from the shells, discarding any clams that failed to open. Add the clam meats to the other seafood.

6 Add the bell peppers, onion, tomatoes, if using, parsley, capers, and gherkins, if using, to the seafood. Drizzle the dressing over the top and then stir gently to mix well. Cover and refrigerate until well chilled, about 3 hours.

7 Transfer to a serving dish and serve chilled.

SPANISH: fino sherry JEREZ, MONTILLA, Albariño/blend GALICIA
NON-SPANISH: unoaked Chardonnay CALIFORNIA, NEW ZEALAND, FRANCE,
             Garganega SOAVE, ITALY

GRIDDLED CLAMS WITH GREEN SAUCE

If you can find razor clams at the market, by all means use them for this recipe. If not, use Manilas or a slightly larger clam. Or, use 8 cleaned squid, opened up flat and cut into triangles. As soon as the squid turn white on the griddle, a matter of moments, transfer to a bowl and spoon on the sauce.

1   If the clams feel gritty, soak them in salted water to cover and refrigerate, stirring them occasionally, for 1 or 2 hours, so they release their sand. Drain well. Or, scrub them clean under running water.

2   In a small bowl, stir together the parsley, green onions, garlic, lemon juice, and oil. If you like a bit of heat, add the chile.

3   Place a griddle or cast-iron pan over high heat. When it is smoking, add the clams and let them steam open, 2 to 3 minutes. Transfer to a shallow bowl. Discard any that failed to open.

4   Spoon the sauce over the clams and serve at once.

SPANISH: Viura/blend RIOJA, CATALONIA, manzanilla sherry JEREZ
NON-SPANISH: Sauvignon Blanc FRANCE, ITALY, SOUTH AFRICA, Sercial MADEIRA

SERVES
4-6

2 pounds clams

¼ cup chopped fresh flat-leaf parsley

2 green onions, including the tender green tops, chopped

2 cloves garlic, finely minced

2 tablespoons fresh lemon juice

½ cup extra virgin olive oil

1 fresh green chile, chopped (optional)

VARIATION

You can also steam the clams, remove the top shell, spoon on some **MOJO VERDE** (page 35) and some toasted bread crumbs, and heat under the broiler or in the oven until the bread crumbs are browned.

FABES CON ALMEJAS

WHITE BEANS WITH CLAMS

SERVES 8

The *fabada*, or white bean stew, is a specialty of Asturias. Usually the stew is made with sausages and ham (see pages 23–24), but this version with clams is one of my favorite tapas. I first tasted it at the Botafumeiro restaurant in Barcelona, and I immediately liked how the briny, salty clam juices worked with the mild, creamy beans. You can also make the dish with mussels in place of the clams. Sometimes I add cooked artichokes to the stew. The beans and artichokes can be cooked the day before and reheated, but wait to steam the clams until just before serving.

Beans

½ pound (generous 1 cup) large dried white beans

1 onion

2 cloves garlic, crushed

1 bay leaf

Salt

2 pounds small clams, preferably Manila

¼ cup extra virgin olive oil, plus more for drizzling

1 onion, chopped

2 cloves garlic, minced

Few saffron threads, warmed and crushed

1 teaspoon red pepper flakes (optional)

2 teaspoons sweet paprika

2 artichokes, cooked, leaves removed, and bottoms cut into eighths (optional)

½ cup dry white wine

Salt and freshly ground black pepper

2 tablespoons chopped fresh flat-leaf parsley

2 tablespoons finely shredded fresh mint

1 TO PREPARE THE BEANS, pick over the beans, discarding any misshapen beans or grit, rinse well, and soak overnight in water to cover. The next day, drain the beans and put them in a saucepan with water to cover by 2 inches. Add the onion, garlic, and bay leaf and bring to a boil over medium heat. Reduce the heat to very low and simmer uncovered, adding 1 to 1½ teaspoons salt after the first 10 minutes of cooking. Cook until the beans are tender, 1 to 1½ hours. Check the beans after 30 minutes to monitor their progress, so they don't overcook and become mushy. Remove the pan from the heat. At this point, you can cover the pan and set it aside for a few hours at room temperature or refrigerate it overnight. Bring to a simmer just before you steam the clams.

2 If the clams feel gritty, soak them in salted water to cover and place in the refrigerator, stirring them occasionally, for 1 or 2 hours, so they release their sand. Drain well. Or, scrub them clean under running water.

3 In a large frying pan, heat the ¼ cup oil over medium heat. Add the onion and cook, stirring occasionally, until softened and translucent, about 10 minutes. Add the garlic, saffron, red pepper flakes, if using, and the paprika and cook, stirring occasionally, for 2 minutes longer. Add the clams, artichokes, if using, and the wine, cover, and cook, shaking the pan occasionally, until the clams open, 3 to 6 minutes (some may be stubborn).

4 Spoon the clams and their juices over the beans, discarding any clams that failed to open, and heat together for 2 minutes. Taste and adjust the seasoning with salt and pepper, keeping in mind the clams may already be salty.

5 Ladle into *cazuelitas* with the clams on top. Sprinkle evenly with the parsley and mint and serve at once.

SPANISH: Godello VALDEORRAS, Chardonnay/blend ALELLA, COSTERS DEL SEGRE
NON-SPANISH: Sémillon/blend AUSTRALIA, WASHINGTON,
　　　　　　　　　Marsanne/Roussanne France, CALIFORNIA, AUSTRALIA

ALMEJAS A LA MARINERA

CLAMS IN WHITE WINE, FISHERMAN'S STYLE

A dish of clams cooked fisherman's style means different things depending on where you are eating on the Spanish coast. It can mean spicy clams cooked with tomato and onion; clams steamed in sherry with a bit of sherry vinegar, as they are at the celebrated Passadís del Pep in Barcelona; or clams cooked in white wine with a hefty measure of garlic, as they are here. Be sure to have some crusty bread on hand for enjoying the delicious juices.

1 If the clams feel gritty, soak them in salted water to cover and refrigerate, stirring them occasionally, for 1 or 2 hours, so they release their sand. Drain well. Or, scrub them clean under running cold water.

2 In a large sauté pan, heat the oil over medium heat. Add the garlic, red pepper flakes, if using, and bread crumbs, and sauté for a few minutes. Add the clams, and then add the wine. Cover and cook, shaking the pan a few times, until the clams open, 3 to 6 minutes (some may be stubborn).

3 Discard any clams that failed to open. Add the vinegar and transfer to a serving dish. Sprinkle with the parsley and serve hot or warm.

SPANISH: Hondarribi TXACOLINA, Verdejo RUEDA
NON-SPANISH: Pinot Grigio ITALY, CALIFORNIA, Sauvignon Blanc CHILE

SERVES

4-6

2 pounds small clams, preferably Manila

⅓ cup extra virgin olive oil

5 cloves garlic, finely minced

Pinch of red pepper flakes (optional)

¼ cup toasted bread crumbs

½ cup dry white wine or dry sherry

Dash of sherry vinegar (optional)

2 tablespoons chopped fresh flat-leaf parsley

ALMEJAS CON JAMÓN CLAMS WITH HAM

The inspiration for this recipe, a Catalan favorite, comes from Cal Pep, which is the little brother of Passadís del Pep. It also combines clams and white wine, but it includes ham as well, in an example of *mar y muntanya*, "sea and mountain," a Catalan favorite. In a large sauté pan, heat 2 to 3 tablespoons olive oil over medium heat. Add 1½ pounds small clams; 3 ounces *serrano* ham, chopped; and 1 fresh chile, chopped, and sauté just until the clams begin to open. Add 2 cloves garlic, chopped; 2 tablespoons chopped fresh flat-leaf parsley; and ¼ cup dry white wine and continue to sauté until the clams open fully. Spoon into a serving dish and accompany with bread.

MEJILLONES Y PATATAS A LA VINAGRETA

MUSSEL AND POTATO SALAD

Mussels are abundant in Galicia, so they are a common tapas bar item. Some cooks serve them in the shell, some on the half shell, and still others shell them and serve them in dishes such as this tasty salad. The chopped fennel adds a pleasant anise flavor and nice crunch, but the salad is also good without it. Garnish the finished dish with chopped hard-boiled eggs and finely minced green and red bell pepper, if desired.

SERVES
4–6

1   Put the potatoes in a saucepan filled with lightly salted water, bring to a boil, reduce the heat to medium, and simmer until tender but still firm when pierced with a knife, about 15 minutes. Drain, immerse immediately in cold water to halt the cooking, and drain again. Cut into halves or quarters and place in a bowl.

2   Arrange the mussels in as flat a layer as possible in a wide saucepan or kettle, discarding any that fail to close to the touch. Add the water, lemon zest, bay leaf, and garlic, cover, and bring to a boil over medium-high heat. Steam, shaking the pan occasionally, just until the mussels open, about 3 minutes.

3   Remove from the heat and discard any mussels that failed to open. When the mussels are cool enough to handle, remove the meats from the shells and discard the shells. To eliminate any sand, strain the cooking liquid through a fine-mesh sieve lined with cheesecloth.

4   Add the warm mussels and the fennel, if using, to the potatoes. In a bowl, whisk together the *alioli* and ½ cup of the strained cooking liquid. Pour the dressing over the salad and toss to mix. Season to taste with salt and pepper, sprinkle with parsley, and serve warm or at room temperature.

SPANISH: Tempranillo/blend LA MANCHA, fino sherry JEREZ
NON-SPANISH: Barbera ITALY, Viognier/blend FRANCE, CALIFORNIA

1 pound tiny new potatoes
   (¾ to 1 inch in diameter)
3 pounds mussels, scrubbed and
   debearded
1 cup water or dry white wine
1 lemon zest strip
1 bay leaf
2 cloves garlic, minced
1 fennel bulb, trimmed, cored, and
   chopped (optional)
1 cup saffron ALIOLI (page 30)
Salt and freshly ground black
   pepper
½ cup chopped fresh flat-leaf
   parsley

CONTINUED

VARIATION

Omit the saffron *alioli*. To make a tomato vinaigrette, in a bowl, whisk together 2 tomatoes, peeled, seeded, and chopped; ½ cup minced red onion; ¼ cup chopped fresh flat-leaf parsley; 6 tablespoons extra virgin olive oil; 2 to 3 table-spoons white wine vinegar; and a pinch of hot paprika or cayenne pepper (optional). Season to taste with salt. Pour over the salad and toss to mix.

SPANISH: rosé RIOJA, VALDEPEÑAS, cava CATALONIA
NON-SPANISH: rosé ITALY, very dry sparkling wine FRANCE, ITALY, PORTUGAL

GAMBAS AL AJILLO

SIZZLING SHRIMP WITH GARLIC

Everyone is familiar with this tapa, and nearly every Spanish cookbook includes a recipe for it. But it is so well liked, I would be foolish to omit it from this chapter. It is typically served sizzling hot in a little metal pan or in a *cazuelita*. Sherry or lemon juice is not always used, but it adds a nice contrast to the richness of the oil and garlic. Some modern chefs add a bit of grated fresh ginger along with the garlic. You can cook squid (bodies cut into ½-inch-wide rings and tentacles left whole), scallops, or clams in this same manner.

SERVES

4

1   In a sauté pan, heat the oil over medium heat. Add the garlic, red pepper flakes to taste, and paprika and cook, stirring, for 1 minute. Add the shrimp, lemon juice, if using, and the sherry, stir well, raise the heat to high, and sauté until the shrimp turn pink and the dish is fragrant, about 3 minutes.

2   Remove from the heat, season with salt and pepper, and transfer to a serving dish or individual dishes. Sprinkle with the parsley and serve at once.

SPANISH: ROSÉ VALENCIA, Godello VALDEORRAS
NON-SPANISH: Vin Gris of Pinot Noir FRANCE, CALIFORNIA, NEW ZEALAND,
      Chardonnay CHABLIS, MACONNAIS, AND CHALONNAIS, FRANCE

¼ cup olive oil

4 cloves garlic, finely minced

½ to 1 teaspoon red pepper flakes

1 teaspoon sweet paprika

1 pound shrimp, peeled and
   deveined

1 to 2 tablespoons fresh lemon juice
   (optional)

2 tablespoons dry sherry or dry
   white wine

Salt and freshly ground black pepper

Chopped fresh flat-leaf parsley for
   garnish

CALAMARES CON GUISANTES

SQUID WITH PEAS

Fish or shellfish combined with peas and mint or peas and parsley appears in many regions. Both are versions of *salsa verde*, a wine-based sauce flavored with green herbs. However, this squid recipe from Catalonia is especially appealing because of the addition of tomatoes and the *picada* enrichment. I also like it because it has a large amount of garlic, but you can use less.

SERVES

8

1 Clean the squid as directed on page 25. Cut the bodies into 1-inch-wide rings. Leave the tentacles whole if small or cut in half if large.

2 If using fresh peas, bring a saucepan filled with salted water to a boil, add the peas, and cook until tender, 3 to 5 minutes. Drain and immediately immerse in cold water to halt the cooking, and then drain again. If using frozen peas, add to boiling salted water and cook only until thawed, or thaw them ahead of time.

3 To make a *picada*, in a large frying pan, heat the oil over medium heat. Add the garlic and sauté until golden, 3 to 4 minutes. Using a slotted spoon, transfer to paper towels to drain. Add the bread to the oil and fry, turning as needed, until crisp and golden on both sides, 5 to 6 minutes. Using the slotted spoon, transfer the bread to paper towels to drain. Reserve the oil in the pan.

4 Combine the garlic and bread in a mortar and pound with a pestle until finely ground. Or, combine in a blender or food processor and pulse until finely ground.

5 Return the frying pan to medium heat and add the flour. When it starts to color, add the tomatoes, wine, garlic-bread mixture, and about half each of the mint and parsley. Stir well and simmer, stirring occasionally, for 15 minutes. If the sauce is too thick, add a little more wine or water. It must have a spoonable consistency. If it is too dry, you will be unable to purée it easily.

CONTINUED

2 pounds squid

4 pounds English peas, shelled (about 4 cups), or about 1¼ pounds frozen peas, thawed

½ cup olive oil

2 small heads garlic, cloves separated and peeled

2 slices country bread, crusts removed

1 tablespoon all-purpose flour

3 tomatoes, peeled, seeded, and chopped

½ cup dry white wine

¼ cup finely shredded fresh mint

¼ cup chopped fresh flat-leaf parsley

6 Transfer to the blender or food processor and process until smooth. If it is still too thick, thin with water. Return the sauce to the pan and bring to a boil over medium-high heat. Add the squid, stir well, and cook until opaque, 1 to 2 minutes. Stir in the peas and heat for 1 minute longer.

7 Transfer to a serving dish and top with the remaining mint and parsley. Serve at once.

SPANISH: Albariño GALICIA, Verdejo RUEDA
NON-SPANISH: Grüner Veltliner AUSTRIA, Sauvignon Blanc NEW ZEALAND, AUSTRALIA

ALMEJAS CON GUISANTES CLAMS WITH PEAS

Omit the squid. Prepare the tomato-garlic sauce as directed, adding the peas to the warm puréed sauce. Scrub 4 pounds clams, place in a large saucepan (discard any that are open or broken), add 1 cup dry white wine, cover, and steam over high heat, shaking the pan occasionally, until the clams open, 3 to 6 minutes. Remove the clams from the pan, leaving the pan juices behind, and add the clams to the sauce. Strain the juices through a fine-mesh sieve lined with cheesecloth, and add to the sauce. Garnish and serve as directed.

CALAMARES RELLENOS

STUFFED SQUID

Squid are enjoyed in tapas bars all over Spain. They may be grilled and dressed with olive oil, lemon juice, and oregano. Other times, they are stuffed and grilled or braised in a sauce of stock and wine or wine and tomatoes. To keep squid tender, you must either cook them for just a few minutes or braise them for a long time. To help ensure tender tendons, use small squid.

SERVES
4-6

1 Clean the squid as directed on page 25. Leave the bodies whole. Chop the tentacles. Prepare a fire in a charcoal or gas grill, or preheat the broiler.

2 In a frying pan, heat the oil over medium heat. Add the onion and cook, stirring occasionally, until softened and translucent, 8 to 10 minutes. Add the garlic, ham, tentacles, and 1 cup bread crumbs, and sauté for 2 minutes, stirring often. Add the lemon juice, parsley, and salt and pepper to taste and mix well. Stir in the egg, remove from the heat, and let the filling cool to room temperature. If the filling seems soupy, add the remaining bread crumbs.

3 Stuff the squid bodies with the filling, being careful not to tear the squid, and skewer the ends closed with a toothpick. Thread the squid onto metal skewers, brush them with olive oil, and sprinkle with salt and pepper.

4 **TO MAKE THE DRESSING**, in a small bowl, whisk together the oil, lemon juice, garlic, oregano, and salt and pepper to taste.

5 Place the skewers on a grill rack, or place on a broiler pan and slip under the broiler. Grill or broil, turning once, until opaque and lightly marked, about 2 to 3 minutes on each side.

6 Slide the squid off the skewers onto a warmed platter, and spoon the dressing over the top. Serve at once.

SPANISH: Albariño GALICIA, Hondarribi TXACOLINA
NON-SPANISH: dry Riesling AUSTRALIA, NEW ZEALAND, Arneis ITALY

12 medium or 16 small squid

¼ cup olive oil

1½ cups chopped onion

4 cloves garlic, minced

½ cup chopped *serrano* ham

1 to 1½ cups fresh bread crumbs

¼ cup fresh lemon juice

6 tablespoons chopped fresh flat-leaf parsley

Salt and freshly ground black pepper

1 egg, lightly beaten

Dressing

⅓ cup extra virgin olive oil

¼ cup fresh lemon juice

1 clove garlic, minced

1 tablespoon dried oregano

Salt and freshly ground black pepper

CONTINUED

BRAISED VARIATION

Omit the dressing. Stuff the squid as directed. In a frying pan, heat 3 tablespoons olive oil over medium heat. Add 2 onions, chopped, and 2 carrots, peeled and chopped, and cook stirring occasionally, until very soft, 15 to 20 minutes. Add 1 bay leaf, 2 cups peeled, seeded, and chopped tomatoes, 1 cup fish stock, and 1 cup dry white wine and bring to a simmer. Add the squid, cover, reduce the heat to low, and cook until the squid are tender, about 1 hour. Remove the squid from the pan, and reduce the pan sauce over high heat as needed to thicken, then season to taste with salt and pepper. Or, thicken the pan juices with a *picada* of ground almonds, sautéed garlic, and saffron.

STUFFING VARIATION WITH PORK OR VEAL

In a sauté pan, heat 2 tablespoons olive oil over medium heat. Add 1 onion, finely chopped, and 1 clove garlic, minced, and sauté until softened and translucent, about 8 minutes. Add ¼ pound ground pork or veal and sauté until the meat is no longer pink, 5 minutes, adding the tentacles during the last 2 minutes of cooking. Transfer to a bowl. Add 2 tablespoons minced fresh flat-leaf parsley, 3 tablespoons toasted chopped pine nuts, and ¾ cup fresh bread crumbs. Season to taste with salt and freshly ground black pepper. Let cool to room temperature.

STUFFING VARIATION WITH SHRIMP AND RICE

In a sauté pan, heat 2 tablespoons olive oil over medium heat. Add the tentacles and ½ pound shrimp, peeled, deveined, and chopped, and sauté until the shrimp are pink and the tentacles are opaque, 1 to 2 minutes. Transfer to a bowl. Add 2 more tablespoons olive oil to the pan over medium heat. Add ½ cup minced onion and 1 clove garlic, minced, until softened and translucent, about 8 minutes. Add ½ cup white rice and 1 cup hot water infused with ¼ teaspoon saffron threads and stir well. Bring to a boil, reduce the heat to low, cover, and cook until the rice has absorbed all of the liquid, about 15 minutes. Return the shrimp and tentacles to the pan and add 2 tablespoons toasted pine nuts, 2 to 3 tablespoons dried currants plumped in hot water (optional), grated zest of 1 large lemon, and 2 tablespoons chopped fresh flat-leaf parsley. Mix well and season to taste with salt and freshly ground black pepper. Let cool to room temperature before stuffing the squid.

CHIPIRONES EN SU TINTA

SQUID COOKED IN THEIR OWN INK

This is a signature dish of Basque cuisine. *Chipirones* are small squid, so seek out the smallest squid you can find for this dish, preferably no more than 3 to 4 inches long. Here, I have created a stuffing that includes the tentacles, but Basque cooks often slip just the tentacles into the bodies.

SERVES

6-8

1 Clean the squid as directed on page 25. Leave the bodies whole. Chop the tentacles.

2 In a sauté pan, heat 2 tablespoons oil over medium heat. Add 1 of the onions and cook, stirring occasionally, until soft and golden, 12 to 15 minutes. Add the tentacles, parsley, and 1 garlic clove. Reduce the heat to low, and stir for 1 minute. Add enough bread crumbs to hold the mixture together and season to taste with salt. Cool to room temperature.

3 Stuff the squid bodies with the filling, being careful not to tear the squid, and skewer the ends closed with a toothpick.

4 In a large sauté pan, heat 3 to 4 tablespoons oil over high heat. Working in batches, sear the stuffed squid on all sides, about 4 minutes for each batch. Transfer to a plate and set aside.

5 Reduce the heat to medium and add the remaining onion and the bell pepper. Cook, stirring occasionally, until the onion is soft and golden, 12 to 15 minutes. Add the remaining garlic and the tomatoes, and cook for a few minutes until slightly reduced. Return the squid to the pan and add the stock and wine, enough to cover the squid. Simmer gently over low heat until the squid is tender, about 45 minutes.

6 Using a slotted spoon, transfer the squid to a plate. Transfer the sauce to a blender or food processor and process until smooth. Return the sauce to the pan off the heat, and stir in the squid ink. Return the squid to the sauce, coat evenly, and reheat gently over low heat. Transfer to a serving dish and serve warm with the grilled bread.

2 pounds small squid (about 2 dozen)

Olive oil

2 onions, chopped

2 tablespoons chopped fresh flat-leaf parsley

4 cloves garlic, minced

1 to 2 tablespoons fresh bread crumbs

Salt

1 red or green bell pepper, seeded and chopped

1 pound tomatoes, peeled, seeded, and chopped

1 cup fish stock

1 cup dry white wine, or as needed

1 tablespoon (about one 4-gram packet) squid ink

Grilled bread for serving

SPANISH: cava CATALONIA, Mencía BIERZO, GALICIA
NON-SPANISH: sparkling wine LIMOUX, ALSACE, AND BURGUNDY, FRANCE, Carménère CHILE

SCALLOPS, GALICIAN STYLE

The scallop shell is the symbol of the Galician pilgrimage town of Santiago de la Compostela and of Saint James the Apostle, whose remains are entombed there. The tale behind how the scallop shell came to symbolize the town and the saint varies, but a common story explains that Saint James rescued a knight from drowning, and when the knight emerged from the water, his armor was covered with scallop shells.

This dish is quite rich, so allow 4 scallops per person. Scallops are often soaked in a solution of tripolyphosphate, which adds to their weight and makes them appear as if they are covered in a milky white liquid. Look for untreated sweet-smelling dry-packed scallops, sometimes labeled diver scallops.

SERVES
4

16 sea scallops, preferably dry pack, tough side muscle removed

1 lemon, halved

6 tablespoons olive oil

1 large onion, finely chopped

2 ounces *serrano* ham or bacon, chopped

1 cup dry white wine

2 teaspoons sweet paprika (optional)

¼ cup chopped fresh flat-leaf parsley

Salt and freshly ground black pepper

½ cup fine dried bread crumbs

1 Preheat the oven to 400°F. Lightly oil 4 *cazuelitas* or shallow ramekins.

2 Divide the scallops evenly among the prepared *cazuelitas* and squeeze a bit of fresh lemon juice over them. Refrigerate until the sauce is ready.

3 In a frying pan, heat the oil over medium heat. Add the onion and ham and cook, stirring occasionally, until the onion is very soft, about 15 minutes. Add the wine and cook until reduced by half, about 5 minutes. Stir in the paprika, if using, and parsley, and season with salt and pepper. Remove from the heat.

4 Spoon the sauce evenly over the scallops, and then sprinkle evenly with the bread crumbs. Bake until the scallops are barely opaque at the center, the sauce is bubbling, and the bread crumbs are golden brown, about 15 minutes. Serve at once.

SPANISH: Albariño/blend GALICIA, Godello VALDEORRAS
NON-SPANISH: Torrontes ARGENTINA, Chardonnay CALIFORNIA, AUSTRALIA

ARROZ NEGRO

CATALAN BLACK RICE

This dish relies on a *sofrito* of tomatoes, onions, garlic, and bell peppers for a deep layer of flavor and on squid ink for its dramatic color. It is often prepared with only squid, but here I have dressed it up with some shrimp and mussels.

SERVES

6

1 Clean the squid as directed on page 25. Cut the bodies into ½-inch-wide rings. Leave the tentacles whole.

2 In a saucepan, heat the stock to just below a simmer. Stir in the squid ink and keep warm.

3 In a large, deep frying pan, heat ¼ cup of the oil over medium heat. Add the onions, garlic, and bell peppers and cook, stirring occasionally, until the onions are softened and translucent, 8 to 10 minutes. Add the tomatoes and cook, stirring occasionally, until they reduce slightly and all of the vegetables are tender, 5 to 8 minutes. Add the rice and stir well to coat. Add the hot stock and season with salt and pepper. Cook over medium-high heat, without stirring, for 10 minutes.

4 While the rice is cooking, put the mussels in a saucepan, discarding any that fail to close to the touch. Add about 1 cup water, cover, and place over high heat. Steam, shaking the pan occasionally, until the mussels open, 3 to 5 minutes. Remove the mussels from the pan, discarding any that failed to open. Strain the cooking liquid through a fine-mesh sieve lined with cheesecloth and reserve. Keep the mussels in their shells.

5 In a sauté pan, heat the remaining ¼ cup oil over medium heat. Add the shrimp and sauté until pink, about 3 minutes. Add the shrimp, cooked mussels and their strained juices, and the squid to the rice and simmer over low heat until the rice is tender, 5 to 10 minutes longer. (Or, place in a preheated 350°F for about 10 minutes to finish the cooking.) Remove from the heat, tent the pan with aluminum foil, and let rest for 5 to 10 minutes before serving.

6 Ladle into individual bowls and serve hot. Pass the *alioli* and lemon wedges.

1 pound squid

5 cups fish stock or water

2 tablespoons (about two 4-gram packets) squid ink

½ cup olive oil

2 onions, chopped

3 or 4 cloves garlic, minced

2 green bell peppers, seeded and finely chopped

1 cup peeled, seeded, and chopped tomatoes

2 cups Spanish rice such as Bomba

Salt and freshly ground black pepper

1 pound mussels, scrubbed and debearded

16 jumbo shrimp, peeled and deveined

ALIOLI (page 30) for serving

Lemon wedges for serving

SPANISH: Cabernet/blend PENEDÈS, NAVARRE, Moristel SOMONTANO
NON-SPANISH: Cabernet/blend BORDEAUX, Pinotage SOUTH AFRICA, NEW ZEALAND

FIDEUÀ

SEAFOOD NOODLES

For this dish, popular in Andalusia and in Catalonia where it is called *rossejat de fideus*, you fry the noodles and then gradually add the broth, much as you do when making risotto. The noodles are called *fideos*, and they look like pieces of vermicelli about 2 inches long. Spaghettini or other thin pasta, broken into short pieces, can be substituted. Some cooks use only shellfish in this dish, and others use only fish. I use a small amount of each.

SERVES

6-8

½ cup olive oil

¾ pound firm white fish fillet, cut into 2-inch pieces

1 onion, chopped

1 green bell pepper, seeded and chopped

6 cloves garlic, crushed

1 pound tomatoes, peeled, seeded, and chopped

¼ cup chopped fresh flat-leaf parsley

1 teaspoon smoked sweet paprika

Generous pinch of ground cinnamon

Salt and freshly ground black pepper

5 cups fish stock

½ teaspoon saffron threads, crushed

½ pound *fideos,* or spaghettini, broken into 2-inch lengths

1 cup dry white wine

1 pound shrimp, peeled and deveined, or clams, scrubbed, or a mixture

ALIOLI (page 30) for serving

Lemon wedges for serving

1   In a large frying pan, heat ¼ cup of the oil over medium-high heat. Add the fish and sauté until lightly colored on both sides but not cooked through, about 4 minutes in all. Using a slotted spoon, set the fish aside on a plate.

2   Add the onion to the oil remaining in the pan and cook over medium heat, stirring occasionally, until softened and translucent, 8 to 10 minutes. Add the bell pepper, 3 of the garlic cloves, and the tomatoes, parsley, paprika, and cinnamon. Stir well and simmer for 10 minutes to blend the flavors. Season to taste with salt and pepper. Remove from the heat.

3   Meanwhile, in a saucepan, combine the stock and saffron and bring to just below a simmer. Keep warm.

4   In a large frying pan, heat the remaining ¼ cup oil over medium heat. Add the *fideos* and the remaining 3 garlic cloves, stir well, and fry, stirring often to prevent the noodles from sticking together, until the noodles take on some color, about 5 minutes. Add the tomato mixture and the wine and cook, stirring, until the wine has evaporated, about 2 minutes. Add 2 cups of the hot broth and cook, stirring occasionally, until the broth has been absorbed. Continue adding the broth, 1 cup at a time, letting the noodles absorb each addition before adding more. You may not need all of the broth.

5 When the noodles are almost tender, after 10 to 12 minutes in all, add the shrimp and/or clams and the fish and cook until the fish is cooked through, the shrimp are pink, and/or the clams have opened, about 5 minutes longer, discarding any clams that failed to open.

6 Transfer the noodles to *cazuelitas* or other individual dishes and serve at once. Pass the *alioli* and lemon wedges.

SPANISH: fino sherry JEREZ, MONTILLA, Treixadura/blend GALICIA
NON-SPANISH: Sercial MADEIRA, Viognier CALIFORNIA, AUSTRALIA

VARIATION

Omit the paprika and cinnamon at the start of cooking and add a *picada* of 2 tablespoons ground toasted almonds; 2 cloves garlic, minced; 2 tablespoons chopped fresh flat-leaf parsley; 1/4 teaspoon saffron threads, warmed and crushed; 1 tablespoon sweet paprika; and 1 teaspoon ground cinnamon at the end when you add the seafood.

If you like, omit the white fish and add 3 pounds clams and 1 pound shrimp.

PULPO A LA GALLEGA

OCTOPUS, GALICIAN STYLE

Fresh octopus is seldom sold in fish markets, but frozen octopus is a good buy because freezing tenderizes the flesh. Most smaller octopus weigh about 2 pounds, or sometimes you can buy just a portion of a larger one. Usually the octopus will have been blanched (if it has, it will be purple) and cleaned.

There are two basic ways to cook octopus. The first is a traditional Spanish technique of shocking it three times in boiling water and then cooking it at a long, slow simmer. Some cooks add a copper penny and others a cork, believing it will help tenderize the flesh. The second technique is to cook it without water, instead allowing it to simmer in its own juices.

This recipe is a specialty of Galicia. The octopus is traditionally combined with cubed potatoes, but it would also be delicious paired with chickpeas. For a touch of color, serve atop a small bed of salad greens.

SERVES
6-8

1 octopus (about 2 pounds), thawed overnight in the refrigerator

1 bay leaf, if boiling the octopus
12 black peppercorns, if boiling the octopus

3 tablespoons extra virgin olive oil, if baking the octopus

1 pound Yukon Gold potatoes, boiled until tender, drained, peeled, and cut into ½-inch cubes, or 2 cups cooked chickpeas
½ cup finely minced red onion
3 cloves garlic, thinly sliced (optional)
½ cup extra virgin olive oil
¼ cup fresh lemon juice or 2 tablespoons each fresh lemon juice and red wine vinegar
Salt
Sweet or hot smoked paprika

1 **IF BOILING THE OCTOPUS**, bring 4 quarts salted water to a boil over high heat and add the bay leaf and peppercorns—and a copper penny or a cork if you are superstitious. Holding the octopus with tongs, dip it into the boiling water 3 times, allowing the water to come back to a boil each time before removing it. Then put the octopus in the pot, reduce the heat to medium, and simmer, uncovered, until the tentacles can be easily pierced (or relatively easily since octopus is rather chewy by nature) with a wooden skewer or toothpick, 1½ to 2 hours. Remove from the heat, let cool in the water, and then remove from the pot with tongs, discarding the cooking liquid. When the octopus is cool enough to handle, cut off and discard the head. Cut the tentacles into ½-inch pieces, and place in a bowl.

IF COOKING THE OCTOPUS IN ITS OWN LIQUID, preheat the oven to 300°F. Place the cleaned octopus in a saucepan with the 3 tablespoons oil. Place over low heat, cover, and cook until the octopus has released its liquid, about 20 minutes. Transfer the octopus and all of the liquid in the saucepan to a baking pan, cover with aluminum foil, and place in the oven. Bake until the tentacles are easily pierced with a wooden skewer or toothpick, 1 to 1½ hours. As the octopus cooks, check from time to time to make sure not all of the liquid has evaporated, adding a little water if the pan begins to look dry. Remove from the oven and let cool until it can be handled. Cut off and discard the head. Cut the tentacles into ½-inch pieces, and place in a bowl.

2 Add the potatoes, onion, and garlic, if using, to the octopus, and then dress with the ½ cup olive oil and the lemon juice, tossing well. Season to taste with salt. Let rest for about 30 minutes to allow the octopus to absorb some of the dressing and to allow the garlic to mellow.

3 Transfer to a serving dish and top with a generous sprinkle of paprika. Serve at room temperature.

SPANISH: Albariño GALICIA, rosé CIGALES
NON-SPANISH: Arneis ITALY, dry rosé ITALY, SOUTHWEST FRANCE

ATÚN A LA PLANCHA

GRIDDLED TUNA

Tuna fishing is important in Galicia, Andalusia, and elsewhere in Spain, so the fish—both preserved and fresh—frequently appears on tapas bar menus. This fresh tuna tapa is so simple and easy—you salt the fish briefly and then sear it quickly—you will be tempted to make it all the time. Some cooks marinate fish in a mixture similar to the spice paste used here and then dust the fish with flour and fry it.

SERVES

6

1 Sprinkle the tuna pieces on both sides with the salt and refrigerate for about 20 minutes. Meanwhile, in a small bowl, combine the pepper, paprika, oregano, and enough oil to make a spreadable thin paste.

2 Preheat a griddle or cast-iron skillet over high heat. Rub the spice paste on one side of each piece of tuna. When the griddle is hot and smoking, add the tuna, spice-side down, and sear until golden about 3 minutes. Flip the pieces and sear on the second sides until golden, about 2 more minutes. The tuna should be almost cooked through but still a bit rare in the center.

3 Transfer the tuna, spice-side up, to a platter and serve at once. Pass the lemon wedges or serve with *samfaina* on the side.

6 pieces tuna fillet (about ¼ pound and ½ inch thick each)

1 teaspoon salt

2 teaspoons freshly ground black pepper

1 teaspoon sweet paprika or sweet smoked paprika

1 teaspoon dried oregano

About 3 tablespoons olive oil

Lemon wedges or SAMFAINA (page 34), optional

SPANISH: Verdejo RUEDA, Sauvignon Blanc/blend CATALONIA, COSTERS DEL SAGRE
NON-SPANISH: Vermentino ITALY, Sauvignon Blanc LOIRE VALLEY, FRANCE; CALIFORNIA

MERLUZA EN SALSA DE PIÑONES

FISH IN PINE NUT SAUCE

Many Spanish fish dishes call for sauces made with almonds, hazelnuts, or pine nuts, sometimes in combination with tomatoes and saffron. While hake or monkfish is traditionally used for this Catalan dish, you can substitute cod, sea bass, flounder, or another firm white fish.

SERVES

8

1 Preheat the oven to 350°F. Spread the pine nuts on a baking sheet and toast in the oven, stirring occasionally, until fragrant and golden, about 8 minutes. Pour onto a plate to cool. Transfer ¼ cup of the toasted nuts to a nut grinder or small food processor and grind or pulse until finely ground.

2 In a frying pan, heat 2 tablespoons of the oil over medium heat. Add the onion and cook, stirring occasionally, until softened and translucent, about 8 minutes. Add the paprika, garlic, ground pine nuts, bread crumbs, and saffron, if using, and cook, stirring often, for 3 minutes. Add the tomatoes and stock and cook, stirring occasionally, until thickened, 5 to 8 minutes. Season to taste with salt and pepper. Keep warm over low heat.

3 In a large frying pan, heat the remaining 2 tablespoons oil over medium heat. Sprinkle the fish with salt and pepper, add to the pan, and cook, turning once, until browned on both sides, about 3 minutes on each side. Pour the sauce over the fish, add the peas, if using, and simmer until the fish is opaque throughout, about 5 minutes longer. Transfer to a serving dish or individual dishes, and garnish with the remaining pine nuts and the parsley. Serve at once.

SPANISH: Chardonnay/blend PENEDÉS, TARRAGONA, dry amontillado sherry JEREZ
NON-SPANISH: Rousanne/blend FRANCE, CALIFORNIA, Chardonnay ARGENTINA, NEW ZEALAND

½ cup pine nuts

4 tablespoons olive oil

1 large onion, finely chopped

1 teaspoon sweet paprika

1 tablespoon finely minced garlic

¼ cup fresh bread crumbs

Pinch of saffron threads, warmed and crushed (optional)

1½ cups peeled, seeded, and chopped tomatoes

1 cup fish stock or dry white wine

Salt and freshly ground black pepper

1½ pounds firm white fish fillet, cut into 8 pieces

1 cup English peas, cooked until tender-crisp (optional)

¼ cup chopped fresh flat-leaf parsley or mint

VARIATION You can skip the step of browning the fish, and instead poach it in the sauce. Or, you can combine the fish and the sauce in a baking dish, making sure the fish is fully covered by the sauce, and bake in a preheated 450°F oven until fish is tender, 10 to 12 minutes, depending on the thickness of the pieces. If baking, do not reduce the sauce too much, as some of the liquid will evaporate in the oven.

MERLUZA A LA SIDRA

HAKE COOKED WITH CIDER

As grapes are hard to cultivate in Galicia and Asturias, and apple trees thrive, it is not surprising that hard cider is used in the local cooking. This dish is usually made with hake or sea bass (*lubina*), but you can instead use cod, flounder, or another mild white fish. Although not every version of the recipe calls for apples, I find they heighten the flavor of the cider.

SERVES

8

1 In a frying pan, heat 2 tablespoons oil over medium heat. Add the onion and garlic and cook, stirring occasionally, until the onion is softened and translucent, about 8 minutes. Add 1 tablespoon flour, the chile, tomatoes, and apples, if using, and stir well. Add the cider, bring to a boil, reduce the heat to low, and simmer until the apples are soft, about 10 minutes. Remove from the heat, let cool slightly, and then transfer to a blender or food processor and process until smooth. Season to taste with salt and pepper. Set aside.

2 Preheat the oven to 450°F.

3 In a large ovenproof sauté pan, heat 4 tablespoons oil over high heat. While the oil is heating, spread a little flour in a shallow bowl. Sprinkle the fish on both sides with salt and then dip in the flour, coating both sides and shaking off the excess. Add the fish to the hot oil and fry, turning once, until browned on both sides, about 4 minutes total. Using a slotted spatula, transfer the fish to a plate and set aside.

4 Add a little more oil to the pan and raise the heat to high. Add the potatoes and fry, turning as needed, until golden on both sides, about 10 minutes. Transfer the potatoes to a *cazuela* or ovenproof baking dish, spreading them in a single or shallow layer. Arrange the fish and clams on top and pour in the cider sauce.

5 Bake until the clams open, the fish is heated through, and the potatoes are tender, about 10 minutes. (Or, cover the pan and finish the cooking on the stove top in about the same amount of time.) Remove from the oven, discard any clams that failed to open, and sprinkle with parsley. Serve at once.

About ½ cup olive oil

1 onion, finely chopped

2 cloves garlic, minced

All-purpose flour as needed

1 small dried hot chile, soaked in water to cover until softened, drained, and stemmed, or 1 teaspoon sweet smoked paprika

2 tomatoes, peeled, seeded, and chopped

2 small apples, peeled, cored, and chopped (optional)

2 cups hard cider

Salt and freshly ground black pepper

1½ pounds firm white fish fillet, cut into 8 pieces

2 large russet potatoes, peeled and sliced ½ inch thick or cut into ½-inch dice

16 clams, scrubbed

Chopped fresh flat-leaf parsley for garnish

SPANISH: Hondarribi TXACOLINA, Chardonnay/blend ALELLA
NON-SPANISH: dry Riesling AUSTRALIA, NEW ZEALAND, Grüner Veltliner AUSTRIA

ESCABECHE

PICKLED FISH

All over Spain, *escabeches* are served as tapas and first courses. Originally made with meat and only rarely with fish (*escabeche* comes from the Arabic *sikbaj*, or "vinegar stew"), today *escabeche* is primarily a dish of pickled fish. Small, oily fish, such as sardines or small mackerel, are traditionally used because they take to the marinade particularly well, developing a smooth, velvety texture. Tuna is also an option. For maximum flavor, let the fish marinate for 2 days before serving. This will also give the vinegar a chance to die down a bit, making the dish more wine friendly. If it is still sharp, serve beer instead.

SERVES

8

3½ pounds fresh sardines or 2 pounds small mackerel fillets or tuna fillet

Kosher salt

All-purpose flour for dusting (optional)

½ cup olive oil

2 white onions, sliced paper-thin

3 cloves garlic, crushed

2 small bay leaves, torn

⅔ cup distilled white vinegar

2 teaspoons salt

1 teaspoon sweet paprika or sweet smoked paprika (optional)

Pinch of saffron threads, warmed and crushed

Pinch of fennel seeds

Freshly ground black pepper

1 lemon, cut into paper-thin slices (optional)

2 to 3 tablespoons chopped fresh flat-leaf parsley (optional)

1 If using sardines or whole mackerel, working with 1 at a time, cut off the head and fins and scrape away the scales. Slit open the belly and remove and discard the viscera, and then slide your fingers inside the belly and carefully lift out and discard the backbone. Rinse well and pat dry. Place the fish fillets on a plate, sprinkle with kosher salt, and let stand for about 15 minutes.

2 If you like, lightly dust the fish on both sides with flour before frying. In a large frying pan, heat 2 tablespoons of the oil over medium heat. Add half of the fish and sauté, turning once, until the fish is golden and tests done when probed with a knife, about 4 minutes total for the sardines or mackerel or 6 minutes for the tuna. Transfer to a plate. Repeat with 2 more tablespoons oil and the remaining fish.

3 In a medium frying pan, heat the remaining 4 tablespoons oil over medium heat. Add the onions and cook, stirring occasionally, until softened and translucent, about 8 minutes. Add the garlic, bay leaves, vinegar, salt, paprika, if using, saffron, fennel seeds, and a few grinds of pepper and let bubble for a minute or two. Remove from the heat and let cool completely. Mix in the lemon slices and parsley, if using.

4 Arrange the fish and onion mixture in alternating layers on a deep platter. Cover with plastic wrap and refrigerate for 2 days before serving.

SPANISH: Verdejo RUEDA, manzanilla sherry JEREZ
NON-SPANISH: Sauvignon Blanc FRANCE, ITALY, Muscadet FRANCE

ATASCABURRAS

SALT COD AND POTATO SPREAD

This dish recalls the classic French dish known as *brandade*, but made without milk. Here, it is served in a bowl and garnished with chopped walnuts and chopped hard-boiled eggs, with bread alongside, but you can also serve it spread on toasted bread and sprinkled with nuts.

SERVES

8-10

1 Place the cod in a bowl with cold water to cover and refrigerate for 24 to 36 hours (the thicker the piece, the longer it will take), changing the water 3 or 4 times.

2 Preheat the oven to 400°F. Pierce the potatoes in a few places, place in the oven, and bake until tender when pierced with a fork, about 1 hour. Remove from the oven, let cool until they can be handled, and then peel and pass the warm potato pulp through a ricer into a bowl, or mash in a bowl with a fork.

3 While the potatoes are baking, drain the cod. In a saucepan, combine the cod with water to cover, bring to a gentle simmer over low heat, and cook until quite tender when pierced with a fork, 10 to 18 minutes. Remove from the heat and drain well, reserving about 1 cup of the cooking water. Let the cod cool until it can be handled, and then break up the cod with your fingers, discarding any errant bones, skin, or tough pieces. Set aside.

4 In a small saucepan, heat the oil until hot, and then remove from the heat.

5 Put the salt cod in a food processor and process until almost a purée. Add the garlic, the hot oil, and enough of the fish cooking water to make a smooth mixture. Fold in the mashed potatoes with a few quick pulses. Do not overprocess or the mixture will become gummy. (You can also use a bowl with a wooden spoon or an immersion blender.) If the mixture is too stiff, whisk in a little more oil or fish cooking water. It needs to be spreadable. Mix in the parsley, lemon juice, and pepper.

6 Mound the mixture on a serving platter or in a wide bowl, and garnish with the walnuts and eggs. Accompany with the bread.

1 pound salt cod fillet

2 russet potatoes, about 1 pound total

1 cup olive oil

1 tablespoon finely minced garlic

½ cup chopped fresh flat-leaf parsley

2 teaspoons fresh lemon juice

Pinch of freshly ground black pepper

1 cup walnuts, toasted and coarsely chopped

3 hard-boiled eggs, peeled and chopped

12 slices country bread, toasted or grilled, for serving

SPANISH: Godello VALDEORRAS, Viura/blend RIOJA, CATALONIA
NON-SPANISH: dry Chenin Blanc FRANCE, SOUTH AFRICA, Alvarinho PORTUGAL

BACALAO A LA VISCAINA

SALT COD, BAY OF BISCAY STYLE

Cooks in neighboring Portugal make a dish similar to this celebrated Basque combination of salt cod with onions and peppers. Its attractive red color comes from the use of *ñora* or other *choricero* peppers (page 22), dried sweet red peppers that also impart a sweet smoky quality to the sauce. If you cannot find *ñoras*, ancho chiles can be used in their place. There are many variations to this recipe. Some cooks add roasted red peppers along with the dried pepper purée. Still others leave the roasted peppers in slices and place them on top of the fish before the fish is baked in the sauce. Diced cooked ham may be used in place of the bacon. (During Lent, both the lard and the bacon—or ham—are omitted.)

SERVES

6

1 Place the cod in a bowl with cold water to cover and refrigerate for 36 to 48 hours (the thicker the piece, the longer it will take), changing the water 3 to 4 times. Drain, reserving some of the soaking water.

2 In a saucepan, combine the cod with water to cover, bring to a gentle simmer over low heat, and cook until quite tender when pierced with a fork, 10 to 18 minutes (the timing depends on the thickness). Drain and let cool until it can be handled, and then cut into 6 equal pieces, discarding any errant skin or visible bones or tough pieces.

3 In a large frying pan, heat the oil over medium heat. Add the bacon, onions, garlic, and parsley and cook, stirring occasionally, until the onions are softened and translucent, about 10 minutes. Stir in the sweet and hot paprika and cook for 1 to 2 minutes. Stir in the pepper purée and/or roasted peppers and cook, stirring occasionally, for about 15 minutes to blend the flavors. Add the bread crumbs and egg yolks, if using, and cook for a few minutes.

4 Remove from the heat, let cool slightly, and then transfer to a blender and process until smooth. If the sauce is too dry, add a bit of the cod soaking water.

1½ pounds salt cod fillet, preferably thick, in 1 or 2 pieces

1 cup olive oil

¼ cup chopped fatty bacon

2 large onions, chopped

4 cloves garlic, minced

¼ cup chopped fresh flat-leaf parsley

1 teaspoon sweet smoked paprika

½ teaspoon hot paprika

¼ cup *ñora* or ancho chile purée (see Note) and/or 2 red bell peppers, roasted, peeled, seeded, and chopped

1 cup fine dried bread crumbs or crushed soda crackers

2 hard-boiled egg yolks, mashed (optional)

4 tablespoons lard or olive oil

Salt and freshly ground black pepper

5 If baking this dish, preheat the oven to 400°F. In a *cazuela*, a flameproof baking dish, or a sauté pan, melt 2 tablespoons of the lard over medium heat. Add a few ladles of the sauce. Place the fish pieces on top, and then ladle the remaining sauce on top. Melt the remaining lard in a small pan and pour over the top. Bake in the oven or simmer gently on the stove top until the cod is heated through, about 15 minutes.

6 Just before serving, taste the sauce and adjust the seasoning with salt and pepper. Serve at once.

SPANISH: Hondarribi TXACOLINA, rosé UTIEL-REQUENA, VALENCIA
NON-SPANISH: Sauvignon Blanc CALIFORNIA, CHILE, Gamay FRANCE

VARIATION

Melt the lard in the *cazuela* as directed, arrange a layer of diced parboiled potatoes in the cazuela, top with the cod pieces, and ladle the sauce over all. Bake as directed until the cod is tender and sauce has reduced a bit, about 25 minutes.

NOTE: To use *ñoras* or ancho chiles, cut off and discard the stems and the loose seeds from 10 *ñoras* or 3 to 4 dried ancho chiles and place in a small saucepan. Add water to cover, bring to a boil, remove from the heat, and let soak until soft, about 1 hour. Drain. Cut the chiles open and discard any remaining seeds. Scrape the pepper pulp from the skins. You should have about ¼ cup. If the peppers have little pulp and are mostly skin, purée the pulp and skin together.

In the past, Spanish cooks valued chickens for the eggs they laid, and although today industrialized poultry farming has made the birds ubiquitous throughout the country, there are relatively few traditional chicken dishes. Indeed, egg recipes, both savory and sweet, far outnumber chicken recipes in the Spanish repertoire. At tapas bars, customers typically find simple chicken preparations, such as *pollo al ajillo*, laced with garlic, or *pollo a la parilla*, grilled with honey. Chicken livers are also a tapas bar treat, here presented in a reduced sherry sauce, as are such small game birds as quail, which are eaten with fingers or more formally with a knife and fork.

Beef plays a minor role in the Spanish tapas kitchen, with *albóndigas*, or "meatballs," its most common form on tapas menus. Lamb, in contrast, has been prized in Spain since Moorish times, and tiny rib chops cooked *a la parilla*—on the grill—are tapas bar favorites today. But above all, Spain is known for its excellent pork, which is grilled, roasted, and braised, as well as salted, cured, and smoked as ham and sausage (see The Spanish Pantry). Its culinary ascendancy occurred after the expulsion of the Moors and Jews, when many traditional lamb dishes were transformed into pork dishes, such as *pinchos morunos*, pork kebabs prepared in the style of the Moors.

In this chapter, you will find only a fraction of the poultry and meat tapas that Spaniards typically encounter in their neighborhood tapas bars, but they are among the most popular. Look in the Shop-and-Serve Tapas section for more ideas.

POULTRY AND MEAT

POLLO AL AJILLO

GARLIC CHICKEN

Here is another popular *al ajillo* preparation. I use chicken thighs for this dish because they remain juicier and are more flavorful than breasts, but chicken wings also work well. If you like a little heat, add a pinch of hot paprika or cayenne pepper with the sherry.

SERVES

4

1 Rub the chicken with the paprika, salt, and pepper and set aside at room temperature for at least 1 hour or in the refrigerator at least 8 hours or overnight.

2 Preheat the oven to 400°F.

3 In a large sauté pan, heat the oil over medium heat. Add the crushed garlic and cook, stirring, until softened but not colored, 2 minutes. Add the chicken pieces and fry, turning as needed, until golden on both sides, 5 to 8 minutes. You want them nicely colored on the outside but not cooked through. Arrange the pieces in a *cazuela* or baking dish large enough to hold them in a single layer.

4 Remove the crushed garlic from the oil and discard. Return the pan to low heat. Add the minced garlic and cook briefly. Add the thyme, bay leaves, sherry, and broth, raise the heat to high, and bring to a boil. Remove from the heat and pour over the chicken.

5 Bake the chicken until cooked through, 25 to 30 minutes. Remove from the oven and discard the bay leaves and thyme. If the pan juices are thin, transfer to a small saucepan and cook over medium-high heat until reduced, and then return to the *cazuela*. Sprinkle with the parsley and serve at once.

4 boneless, skinless chicken thighs, cut into 1½-inch pieces, or 12 chicken wings, tips removed

Sweet paprika

Salt and freshly ground black pepper

⅓ cup olive oil

6 cloves garlic, crushed, plus 2 cloves, minced

3 fresh thyme sprigs

2 bay leaves

½ cup fino or manzanilla sherry

½ cup chicken broth

Chopped fresh flat-leaf parsley for garnish

SPANISH: rosé CAMPO DE BORJA, NAVARRE, Tempranillo/blend RIOJA, CATALONIA
NON-SPANISH: rosé RHÔNE VALLEY AND PROVENCE, FRANCE, Pinot Noir OREGON, FRANCE, NEW ZEALAND

VARIATION

You also can complete the cooking on the stove top. Sauté the minced garlic as directed, return the chicken to the pan, add the sherry and broth, and simmer, uncovered, until most of the liquid has evaporated and the chicken is tender, 15 to 20 minutes.

POLLO A LA PARILLA CON MIEL Y COMINO

GRILLED CHICKEN WITH HONEY AND CUMIN

This classic sweet-and-sour, or *agridulce*, chicken recipe is similar to many early Roman dishes. What makes it Spanish is the use of cumin, part of the Moorish legacy, and the sherry vinegar. You can also make this dish with quail, which can be easily cut into halves for sharing. Instead of simply brushing the sauce on the meat as it cooks, I marinate it overnight and then grill it, basting from time to time.

SERVES
8–12

1 In a small saucepan, combine the honey, oil, vinegar, cumin, garlic, and pepper and warm over low heat until hot. Taste and adjust the balance of flavors to create a good sweet-and-sour taste, as different brands of honey and sherry vinegar vary in intensity. Remove from the heat and let cool completely. Measure out ¼ cup of the marinade and set aside for basting.

2 Place the chicken or quail in a shallow dish, pour the marinade over the top, turn to coat evenly, cover, and refrigerate overnight. Bring to room temperature before cooking.

3 Prepare a fire in a charcoal or gas grill, or preheat the broiler.

4 Remove the chicken or quail from the marinade, and sprinkle with salt. If using chicken, place it skin-side down on the grill rack, or place it skin-side up on a broiler pan and slip under the broiler. Cook for 5 to 6 minutes, basting a few times. Turn the chicken over and cook, again basting a few times, until opaque throughout, 3 to 5 minutes longer. If using quail, cook breast-down on the grill and breast-up on the broiler for 4 to 5 minutes, basting a few times, and then turn and cook on the other side for 4 to 5 minutes longer, again basting a few times. Do not be alarmed if the skin turns quite dark—almost black. It means the honey is caramelizing, which will taste great.

5 Transfer to a platter and serve at once with the *alioli*, if using.

½ cup honey

¾ cup olive oil

3 tablespoons sherry vinegar

2 tablespoons cumin seeds, toasted in a dry pan until fragrant and finely ground

1 tablespoon finely minced garlic

1 teaspoon freshly ground black pepper

16 small chicken thighs or drumsticks or 8 quail, preferably boned

Salt

Quince or apple ALIOLI (optional; page 30)

SPANISH: Garnacha/blend CAMPO DE BORJA, CATALYUD, MONSANT,
  dry amontillado sherry JEREZ
NON-SPANISH: Grenache/blend FRANCE, NORTH AFRICA, CALIFORNIA,
  Gewürztraminer FRANCE, NEW ZEALAND, CALIFORNIA

CORDONICES EN HOJA DE PARRA

QUAIL IN GRAPE LEAVES

Once you have found the quail, this recipe is easy to prepare. The birds can be cooked in the oven, grilled over charcoal, or braised on top of the stove. In summer, when figs are abundant, omit the thyme sprigs and lemon zest and slip a fig half—never a whole fig, which might explode—inside each quail.

SERVES
8

1   Rub the quail inside and out with salt and pepper. Stuff 1 thyme sprig and 1 lemon zest strip in each bird, and then wrap each bird in 2 grape leaves, overlapping them to cover completely. Finally, wrap a ham strip around each quail. Secure the leaves and ham in place with kitchen string or toothpicks.

2   Preheat the oven to 400°F.

3   In a large sauté pan, heat the oil over high heat. Working in batches, add the quail and sear on all sides until well browned. Transfer to a *cazuela* or flameproof baking pan and drizzle the broth around the birds. Roast in the oven until the quail test done, 12 to 15 minutes. Discreetly cut into 1 quail with a knife to check for doneness. They are best served medium-rare or medium. Transfer the quail to a heated platter and snip the strings.

4   Place the *cazuela* on the stove top over medium heat, add the sherry, and deglaze, scraping the bottom with a wooden spatula to dislodge any browned bits. Reduce the pan juices slightly and then spoon over the quail. Serve the quail at once with the bread.

8 quail, preferably boned

Salt and freshly ground black pepper

8 fresh thyme sprigs

8 lemon zest strips

16 brined grape leaves, rinsed and stems removed

8 long strips *serrano* ham or bacon

2 tablespoons olive oil

½ cup chicken broth

½ cup dry fino sherry

Country bread, grilled or fried in olive oil, for serving

SPANISH: Monastrell JUMILLA, YECLA, Mencía BIERZO, GALICIA
NON-SPANISH: Merlot WASHINGTON, Pinotage SOUTH AFRICA

VARIATION

To grill the quail, prepare a fire in a charcoal or gas grill. Season and wrap the birds as directed, then brush with olive oil, flavored with a little anisette if desired. Cook the quail over the fire, turning as needed, until they are browned on both sides and test done, about 5 minutes on each side. Or, to cook on the stove top, season, wrap, and sear the birds as directed. Add the broth, cover, and cook over medium heat until the birds test done, 12 to 15 minutes.

CORDONICES CON MANZANAS

QUAIL WITH APPLES

This recipe comes from Asturias, where apple orchards are more numerous than vineyards and nearly everyone drinks the locally made carbonated hard cider. I like to add chorizo, but you can serve the quail with just the apples and raisins.

SERVES

8–12

1 In a small bowl, whisk together the ½ cup oil, vinegar, garlic, and salt and pepper to taste. Place the quail in a shallow dish, pour the oil mixture over them, turn the quail to coat evenly, and set aside at room temperature for 1 hour. In a small bowl, soak the raisins in the brandy for 30 minutes to plump.

2 Prick the chorizos and place in a frying pan. Add cider to a depth of about ¾ inch, place over medium heat, and cook, turning occasionally, until cooked through, about 10 minutes. Remove from the heat and let cool slightly. Cut into chunks and set aside.

3 In large sauté pan, heat the 3 tablespoons oil over high heat. Add the quail in batches and sear on all sides until well browned. Remove from the pan. Reduce the heat to low, and add the carrot, celery, and onion. Cook, stirring occasionally, until the vegetables are golden, 15 to 20 minutes. Add the broth and sherry, raise the heat to medium-high, and bring to a boil. Return the quail to the pan, cover, and cook over low heat until the quail test done, 10 to 15 minutes. They are best served medium-rare or medium. Add the sausage pieces during the last 5 minutes of cooking to heat through.

4 In another sauté pan, melt the butter over medium heat. Add the apples and sauté until softened, 5 to 8 minutes. Sprinkle the sugar over the apples, stir, and raise the heat to high. When the sugar caramelizes, after about 3 minutes, add the raisins and brandy and ignite with a match. Let the flames die down.

5 Transfer the quail and sausages to a platter. Strain the pan juices through a fine-mesh sieve over the apples. Cook over high heat until reduced and syrupy. Surround the quail with the sautéed apples. Spoon the sauce over the quail and serve.

½ cup olive oil, plus 3 tablespoons

¼ cup moscatel vinegar or balsamic vinegar

2 cloves garlic, minced

Salt and freshly ground black pepper

8 quail, preferably boned

¾ cup raisins

½ cup brandy or anisette

2 semidry chorizos (about ½ pound total weight)

About 1 cup hard cider or water

1 carrot, peeled and chopped

1 celery stalk, chopped

1 onion, chopped

1 cup chicken broth

1 cup dry amontillado or fino sherry

3 tablespoons unsalted butter

2 pounds tart apples (about 4), peeled, halved, cored, and cut into wedges

¼ cup sugar

SPANISH: Albariño GALICIA, fino sherry JEREZ
NON-SPANISH: Chenin Blanc FRANCE, SOUTH AFRICA, CALIFORNIA, Riesling GERMANY, WASHINGTON, NEW YORK

HIGADILLOS AL JEREZ

CHICKEN LIVERS WITH SHERRY

Fast, easy, and tasty, this dish is for anyone who likes chicken livers. Serve it with lots of bread for mopping up the sauce. As a variation, marinate the livers in the sherry for an hour, thread the livers on skewers, and broil them, basting with the sherry.

SERVES

8

1 Clean the livers well, trimming away any veins, fat, and discolored areas, and separate the lobes. Pat the livers dry. Sprinkle with salt and pepper.

2 Film the bottom of a large sauté pan with oil and heat over high heat. Add the livers and sauté quickly, turning once, until crusty and browned on the outside and medium-rare to pink in the middle, about 5 minutes total. Transfer the livers to a plate and keep warm.

3 Pour the sherry into the pan over high heat and deglaze, scraping up any browned-on bits from the pan bottom with a wooden spatula. Reduce the sherry until thickened and syrupy.

4 Return the livers to the pan and quickly turn to coat with the pan sauce. Transfer to a serving dish and serve with toothpicks.

1 pound chicken livers
Salt and freshly ground black pepper
Olive oil for sautéing
1 cup sweet sherry such as oloroso

 SPANISH: oloroso sherry JEREZ, MÁLAGA, Garnacha PRIORAT
NON-SPANISH: Carignan/blend BANYULS, FRANCE,
Corvina/blend VALPOLICELLA AND AMARONE, ITALY

VARIATION

Sauté the livers as directed and set aside. Return the pan to medium heat and add 1 tablespoon olive oil. Add 3 shallots, chopped, and sauté for 1 to 2 minutes. Add 2 tablespoons sherry vinegar, ¼ cup fino sherry, and ½ cup chicken broth, bring to a boil, deglaze the pan, and reduce until syrupy. Return the livers to the pan, coat with the sauce, and sprinkle with chopped fresh thyme and flat-leaf parsley. Serve as directed.

ALBÓNDIGAS

MEATBALLS WITH TWO SAUCES

The Spanish word *albóndiga*, or "meatball," comes from the Arabic *al bundaq*, or "round." I have included bread in the meat mixture because it yields a lighter meatball, but not all Spanish cooks add it. You can fry the meatballs and serve them plain, with ALIOLI (page 30) on the side, or in an almond-thickened wine sauce, or you can brown them only and finish them in a cinnamon-scented tomato sauce.

1 If onion is too assertive for your palate, heat 2 tablespoons oil in a small frying pan over low heat, add the onion and garlic, and cook, stirring occasionally, until softened, about 3 minutes. Remove from the heat and let cool completely. Alternatively, combine the raw onion and garlic with the other ingredients as follows.

2 In a bowl, combine the onion, garlic, meat, parsley, egg, soaked bread, nutmeg, and cumin, if using, and season with salt and pepper. Mix well. Fry a nugget of the mixture in a little oil, taste, and adjust the seasoning if necessary.

3 Dampen your hands and shape the meat mixture into 1-inch balls. (At this point, the meatballs can be covered and refrigerated for up to 8 hours before frying.) Spread the flour in a shallow bowl. One at a time, roll the meatballs in the flour, coating evenly and shaking off the excess.

4 In a large frying pan, heat 3 tablespoons oil over medium-high heat. Working in batches to avoid crowding, add the meatballs and sear, turning and adding oil as needed, until golden on all sides and cooked through, about 10 minutes for each batch. Transfer to a plate and serve with toothpicks.

Alternatively, brown the meatballs (about 5 minutes) but do not cook them through, and then simmer them until fully cooked in the wine sauce or tomato sauce. Transfer to a deep platter or *cazuela* and serve with toothpicks.

CONTINUED

SERVES
8

Olive oil

¼ cup minced or grated onion (optional)

2 cloves garlic, finely minced

½ pound each ground beef and ground pork or 1 pound ground beef

3 tablespoons finely minced fresh flat-leaf parsley

1 large egg, lightly beaten

2 slices country bread (about 2 ounces), crusts removed, soaked in water and squeezed dry

½ teaspoon freshly grated nutmeg or ground cinnamon

1 teaspoon cumin seeds, toasted in a dry pan until fragrant and finely ground (optional)

Salt and freshly ground black pepper

About ½ cup all-purpose flour

(Optional)
Wine Sauce (page 152) or Tomato Sauce (page 152)

1 Brown the meatballs for about 5 minutes as directed and set aside. To make a *picada*, in a small food processor, combine the garlic, almonds, parsley, paprika, saffron, a pinch or two of salt, and a few grinds of pepper and process until finely ground. Set aside.

2 In a large frying pan, heat the oil over medium heat. Add the onion and cook, stirring occasionally, until softened and translucent, about 8 minutes. Add the wine and broth and bring to a simmer. Add the meatballs, reduce the heat to low, cover, and simmer until cooked through, 8 to 10 minutes. Add the *picada* and cook for a few minutes longer. Season to taste with salt and pepper. Serve as directed.

SPANISH: dry amontillado sherry JEREZ, Godello VADEORRAS
NON-SPANISH: Marsanne/blend RHÔNE VALLEY, FRANCE; CALIFORNIA,
aged Chardonnay CALIFORNIA, AUSTRALIA

Wine Sauce

2 cloves garlic, minced

2 tablespoons chopped blanched almonds

2 tablespoons chopped fresh flat-leaf parsley

½ teaspoon sweet paprika

Few saffron threads, warmed and crushed

Salt and freshly ground black pepper

2 tablespoons olive oil

½ cup minced onion

½ cup dry white wine or dry fino or amontillado sherry

⅔ cup chicken broth

Brown the meatballs for about 5 minutes as directed and set aside. Add the onion and garlic to the oil remaining in the pan and cook over medium heat, stirring occasionally, until softened, about 8 minutes. Add the tomatoes, season with salt and pepper, and stir well. Add the cinnamon and honey and simmer over medium heat until the tomatoes give off their juices and the sauce thickens, about 15 minutes. Return the meatballs to the pan, reduce the heat to low, cover, and simmer until the meatballs are cooked through, 8 to 10 minutes. Taste and adjust the seasoning. Sprinkle with the parsley before serving as directed.

SPANISH: Tempranillo/blend RIOJA, VALDEPEÑAS, NAVARRE, rosé ALICANTE, UTIEL-REQUENA
NON-SPANISH: Sangiovese/blend ITALY, dry rosé CALIFORNIA, AUSTRALIA

Tomato Sauce

1 small onion, minced

2 cloves, garlic, minced

4 large tomatoes, peeled, seeded, and chopped (2½ to 3 cups)

Salt and freshly ground black pepper

¼ teaspoon ground cinnamon, or to taste

1 tablespoon honey

2 tablespoons chopped fresh flat-leaf parsley

ALBÓNDIGAS DE CORDERO CON HIERBABUENA

LAMB MEATBALLS WITH MINT

This recipe is adapted from a tapa served at Seville's Enrique Becerra restaurant, a favorite of locals and visitors alike. You can also fry the meatballs until fully cooked and serve them with ALIOLI (page 30) for dipping, or fry them until fully cooked, and serve the sauce on the side for dipping.

SERVES

8

Meatballs

1 pound ground lamb

4 to 5 tablespoons fresh bread crumbs

½ onion, grated

2 cloves garlic, minced

2 teaspoons cumin seeds, toasted in a dry pan until fragrant and finely ground

3 tablespoons finely chopped fresh mint

2 teaspoons grated lemon zest (optional)

1 large egg, lightly beaten

Salt and freshly ground black pepper

About ½ cup all-purpose flour

Olive oil

Sauce

¼ cup olive oil

2 onions, chopped

2 cloves garlic, minced

½ cup dry fino sherry or dry white wine

1 cup tomato purée

½ cup lamb or beef broth or water

Salt and freshly ground black pepper

1 tablespoon finely shredded fresh mint

1 **TO MAKE THE MEATBALLS**, in a bowl, combine the lamb, bread crumbs, onion, garlic, cumin, mint, lemon zest, if using, and egg, and season with salt and pepper. Mix well.

2 Dampen your hands and shape the meat mixture into 1-inch balls. (At this point, the meatballs can be covered and refrigerated for up to 8 hours before frying.) Spread the flour in a shallow bowl. One at a time, roll the meatballs in the flour, coating evenly and shaking off the excess. Set on a plate.

3 **TO MAKE THE SAUCE**, in a sauté pan, heat the oil over medium heat. Add the onions and cook, stirring occasionally, until translucent, 8 to 10 minutes. Add garlic and cook for 2 minutes longer. Add the sherry and cook until reduced by half. Add the tomato purée and broth and simmer for 5 minutes to blend the flavors. Let cool slightly, and then transfer to a blender and process until smooth. Return the sauce to the pan, season with salt and pepper, and stir in the mint. Reserve in the pan off the heat.

4 In a large frying pan, heat 3 tablespoons oil over medium-high heat. Working in batches to avoid crowding, add the meatballs and sear, turning and adding oil as needed, until golden on all sides, about 5 minutes for each batch.

5 Bring the sauce to a simmer over medium heat, add the meatballs, reduce the heat to low, and simmer until cooked through, 8 to 10 minutes. Transfer to a deep platter or *cazuela* and serve hot or warm with toothpicks.

SPANISH: Mencía BIERZO; RIBEIRA SACRA, GALICIA,
Cabernet/blend RIBERA DEL DUERO, CATALONIA
NON-SPANISH: Syrah/blend WASHINGTON; NORTH RHÔNE VALLEY, FRANCE,
Cabernet/blend CHILE, SOUTH AFRICA, ARGENTINA

BABY LAMB CHOPS WITH HONEY AND SHERRY VINEGAR

Nowadays, many markets carry racks of baby lamb chops, making this simple, tasty tapa—the perfect finger food—an easy one to assemble. You will need to plan ahead, however, as the chops must marinate for at least a day. If short on time, skip the marinating step, brush the chops with olive oil, sprinkle with salt and pepper, grill, and serve with quince or apple ALIOLI (page 30) or SALSA ROMESCO (page 32).

SERVES

8

2 racks baby lamb chops, about 8 chops each, 2½ to 3 pounds total weight

¼ cup dry amontillado sherry

½ cup olive oil

¼ cup chopped fresh mint

5 tablespoons honey

2 tablespoons Dijon mustard

1 tablespoon cumin seeds, toasted in a dry pan until fragrant and finely ground

Salt and freshly ground black pepper

1   Cut the lamb racks into individual chops and arrange in a single layer in a shallow dish. Refrigerate or keep at room temperature until the marinade is cool.

2   Combine the sherry and oil and warm over low heat until hot. Add the mint, remove from the heat, and let stand until cooled to room temperature to develop the flavor. Then whisk in the honey, mustard, cumin, and salt and pepper to taste. Measure out ¼ cup of the mixture and set aside to use for basting the chops. Pour the remaining mixture over the chops, turn to coat evenly, cover, and refrigerate for at least 24 hours or up to 48 hours. Bring to room temperature before grilling.

3   Prepare a fire in a charcoal or gas grill, or preheat the broiler.

4   Remove the chops from the marinade and sprinkle with salt and pepper. Place on the grill rack, or arrange on a broiler pan and slip under the broiler. Grill or broil, turning once and basting a few times with the reserved marinade, 3 to 4 minutes on each side for rare or medium-rare.

5   Transfer the chops to a platter and serve at once.

SPANISH: Tempranillo/blend TORO, RIBERA DEL DUERO, CASTILE AND LEÓN, Garnacha PRIORAT, MONSANT. JUMILLA
NON-SPANISH: Nebbiolo ITALY, Pinot Noir FRANCE, CALIFORNIA

PINCHOS MORUNOS

PORK KEBABS, IN THE STYLE OF THE MOORS

Here is an example of Christian Spain adapting the flavors of Moorish Spain to their favorite meat. Originally made with lamb, these spicy pork morsels are served at tapas bars all over Spain. To dress up this classic in summertime, brush peach halves with some of the marinade and grill them along with the kebabs. I like to use pork tenderloins for this recipe because they are a good size and are tender.

SERVES

8

1   In a small saucepan, combine the oil, cumin, sweet and hot paprika, saffron infusion, oregano, 1 teaspoon salt, and the pepper and warm over low heat for 3 to 4 minutes to release the aromas of the seasonings. Remove from the heat and let cool to room temperature.

2   Place the pork in a bowl and rub with the oil mixture, coating evenly. Add the garlic, parsley, and lemon juice and toss well. Cover and refrigerate overnight. Bring to room temperature before cooking.

3   Soak bamboo skewers in water to cover for 30 minutes. Prepare a fire in a charcoal or gas grill, or preheat the broiler.

4   Drain the skewers. Remove the pork from the marinade, thread onto the skewers, and sprinkle with salt. Place on the grill rack, or arrange on a broiler pan and slip under the broiler. Grill or broil, turning once, until just cooked through, about 4 minutes on each side.

5   Serve the skewers with lemon wedges.

SPANISH: Tempranillo/blend RIOJA, LA MANCHA, CATALONIA,
       Cabernet/blend PENEDÈS, COSTERS DEL SEGRE
NON-SPANISH: Barbera ITALY, Merlot/blend FRANCE, CHILE, WASHINGTON

½ cup olive oil

2 tablespoons cumin seeds, toasted in a dry pan until fragrant and finely ground

1 tablespoon sweet paprika

½ to 1 teaspoon hot paprika

½ teaspoon saffron threads, crushed and steeped in 2 tablespoons hot water

2 teaspoons dried oregano

Salt

½ teaspoon freshly ground black pepper

2 pounds pork tenderloin, cut into 1-inch pieces

2 tablespoons minced garlic

2 tablespoons chopped fresh flat-leaf parsley

¼ cup fresh lemon juice

Lemon wedges for serving

LOMO EN ADOBO

PORK MARINATED IN PAPRIKA AND GARLIC

This recipe, more formally called *lomo de cerdo adobado*, is a Spanish classic. I learned how to make it from Tomás Herranz, who heads up the kitchen at El Cenador del Prado in Madrid, when he was a guest chef at my one-time restaurant, Square One. Like many talented cooks, he didn't measure precisely, nor did he work from a written recipe. He knew this dish by heart and by palate. My recipe is based on taste memory and a little research. You can also serve the sliced meat on toasted bread or in a *boccadillo* spread with either of the sauces included here.

SERVES
8–10

1 In a small saucepan, combine 3 tablespoons of the oil, the garlic, and oregano and warm over low heat for 2 to 3 minutes to release the aromas of the seasonings. Remove from the heat, whisk in the paprika, cumin, sherry, 1 teaspoon salt, and ½ teaspoon pepper, and let cool to room temperature.

2 Place the pork in a shallow dish, pour the cooled oil mixture over the top, and then rub the oil into the meat. Cover and refrigerate overnight or for up to 2 days.

3 Prepare a fire in a charcoal or gas grill, or preheat the broiler.

4 Remove the pork from the marinade and sprinkle lightly with salt and pepper. Place on the grill rack, or place on a broiler pan and slip under the broiler. Grill or broil, turning the meat occasionally, until just cooked through, about 10 minutes in all for tenderloins and about 18 minutes for the boneless loin, or until an instant-read thermometer inserted into the thickest part registers 140°F.

5 Transfer the pork to a platter and let rest for 5 minutes. Then slice thinly and serve with the *alioli*.

SPANISH: Tempranillo/blend RIOJA, NAVARRE, dry amontillado sherry JEREZ
NON-SPANISH: Pinot Noir OREGON, NEW ZEALAND, Carignan/blend FRANCE, CALIFORNIA

6 tablespoons olive oil

1½ tablespoons finely minced garlic

2 teaspoons dried oregano

2 tablespoons sweet paprika or sweet smoked paprika

1 tablespoon cumin seeds, toasted in a dry pan until fragrant and finely ground

½ cup fino sherry or dry white wine

Salt and freshly ground pepper

2 pounds pork tenderloin or boneless pork loin, well trimmed

Apple or quince ALIOLI (page 30) or SALSA ROMESCO (page 32)

CONTINUED

VARIATIONS

Pound pork loin slices to a thickness of about ¼ inch, combine with the marinade, and refrigerate for at least 3 hours or up to overnight. Sandwich a slice of Manchego cheese between 2 slices of marinated pork, dip in flour, then in beaten egg, and finally in bread crumbs, and fry in olive oil until golden on both sides and the cheese has begun to melt.

You can also cut the pork loin into thin slices, combine with the marinade, refrigerate for 3 to 4 hours, and then grill or fry in olive oil. Or sear the whole tenderloins or pork loin on all sides in olive oil on the stove top and then finish the cooking in a 350°F oven.

CARNE EN SALSA DE ALMENDRAS

PORK IN ALMOND SAUCE

Do not let the amount of garlic in this typical Catalan tapa scare you off. The whole head flavors the sauce but may be discarded after cooking. The flavorful almond *picada* both thickens and enriches the sauce. Accompany the pork with crusty bread for mopping up the robust sauce.

SERVES

8

1 To make a *picada*, heat the oil in a large sauté pan over medium high heat. Add the almonds and fry until golden, about 4 minutes. Using a slotted spoon, transfer the almonds to a plate. Add the bread to the oil remaining in the pan and fry, turning once, until golden on both sides, about 4 minutes total. Transfer the bread to the plate with the almonds. Add the 4 garlic cloves to the oil remaining in the pan and sauté just until barely colored. Add to the almonds and bread and set aside.

2 Add the pork to the oil remaining in the pan over medium-high heat and sauté until lightly colored, about 8 minutes. Add the halved garlic head, onions, tomato, bay leaves, paprika, and wine and bring to a boil. Reduce the heat to low, cover, and simmer for 25 to 30 minutes.

3 Using the slotted spoon, transfer the pork to a plate and set aside. Remove and discard the garlic halves and bay leaves. Again using the slotted spoon, transfer the onion and tomato halves to a blender or food processor and add the reserved almonds, bread, garlic cloves, and a little of liquid from the pan. Process until smooth. If you are in love with garlic, you can squeeze the softened cloves from the cooked garlic halves into the sauce.

4 Pour the purée into the liquid remaining in the pan and then return the pork to the pan. Place over medium heat and simmer, uncovered, until the sauce is reduced and the meat is completely tender, 10 to 15 minutes longer. If the sauce thickens too much before the pork is tender, add water as needed to thin.

5 Taste and adjust the seasoning with salt and pepper and transfer to a serving dish. Serve at once.

6 tablespoons olive oil

½ cup (2 ounces) blanched almonds

1 slice country bread, crust removed

4 cloves garlic, plus 1 head, halved crosswise

2 pounds pork shoulder, cut into 1-inch cubes

2 small onions, halved

1 large tomato, halved

2 bay leaves

2 teaspoons sweet paprika

2 cups dry white wine or 1 cup each dry white wine and meat or poultry broth

Salt and freshly ground black pepper

SPANISH: Tempranillo/blend LA MANCHA, RIOJA, CIGALES, Chardonnay/blend PENEDÉS, TARRAGONA

NON-SPANISH: aged Cabernet/blend FRANCE, CALIFORNIA, Torrontes ARGENTINA

FABADA ASTURIANA

WHITE BEANS WITH MEAT, ASTURIAN STYLE

Fabada has been described as a pig resting on a bed of beans. Asturias is known for its fine *fabes de las Granjas*, white beans that are used to make this iconic dish. If you cannot find them, use white runner beans like Coronas, large limas, or Great Northerns. The *morcillas*, blood sausages flavored with onion, are sweet and delicious, but you can omit them and include only the chorizos, increasing the number to six sausages. Serve this tapa in a large *cazuela* to share, or divide among *cazuelitas*, making sure everyone gets an equal amount of the sausage.

1 Pick over the beans, discarding any misshapen beans or grit, rinse well, and soak overnight in water to cover. The next day, drain the beans and place in a saucepan wide enough to hold all of the meats in a single layer. Add the garlic, onion, bay leaf, bacon, ham, sausages, and water to cover by 2 inches. Bring to a boil over medium heat. In Asturia, cooks traditionally add a glass of cold water at this point, which is said to shock the beans and thus keep them from splitting, and then bring them back to a boil. Reduce the heat to low, cover partially, and simmer for 1 hour.

2 Add the paprika, cinnamon, saffron, and cabbage, if using, re-cover partially, and simmer until the cabbage is tender, 30 minutes to 1 hour longer. Taste and adjust the seasoning with salt and pepper.

3 Remove the meats from the pan, slice, and then return them to the pan and mix with the beans. Transfer to a serving dish and sprinkle with the parsley. Serve at once.

SPANISH: Garnacha/blend MONSANT, CATALAYUD, Tempranillo/blend CASTILE AND LEÓN, RIOJA

NON-SPANISH: Grenache/blend FRANCE, AUSTRALIA, Zinfandel CALIFORNIA

SERVES
8-10

- 1 pound dried large white beans
- 8 cloves garlic
- 1 onion
- 1 bay leaf
- ¼ pound bacon, in a single piece
- 5-ounce slice *serrano* ham, or 1 small ham hock, soaked for 3 hours
- 3 semicured chorizos (about ¾ pound total weight)
- 3 *morcillas* (about ¾ pound total weight)
- 2 teaspoons sweet paprika or sweet smoked paprika
- ½ teaspoon ground cinnamon
- Generous pinch of saffron threads, warmed and crushed
- 1 Savoy cabbage, cut into quarters, cored, and coarsely shredded (optional)
- Salt and freshly ground black pepper
- 2 to 3 tablespoons chopped fresh flat-leaf parsley or finely shredded fresh mint

INDEX

TABLE OF EQUIVALENTS

The exact equivalents in the following tables have been rounded for convenience.

Liquid/Dry Measurements

U.S.	Metric
¼ teaspoon	1.25 milliliters
½ teaspoon	2.5 milliliters
1 teaspoon	5 milliliters
1 tablespoon (3 teaspoons)	15 milliliters
1 fluid ounce (2 tablespoons)	30 milliliters
¼ cup	60 milliliters
⅓ cup	80 milliliters
½ cup	120 milliliters
1 cup	240 milliliters
1 pint (2 cups)	480 milliliters
1 quart (4 cups, 32 ounces)	960 milliliters
1 gallon (4 quarts)	3.84 liters
1 ounce (by weight)	28 grams
1 pound	448 grams
2.2 pounds	1 kilogram

Lengths

U.S.	Metric
⅛ inch	3 millimeters
¼ inch	6 millimeters
½ inch	12 millimeters
1 inch	2.5 centimeters

Oven Temperature

Fahrenheit	Celsius	Gas
250	120	½
275	140	1
300	150	2
325	160	3
350	180	4
375	190	5
400	200	6
425	220	7
450	230	8
475	240	9
500	260	10